Harmony at Hand

Navigating Work-Life Balance in Post-Pandemic Times

by
Well-Being Publishing

Copyright 2023 Well-Being Publishing. All rights reserved.

WELL-BEING
PUBLISHING

No part of this book may be reproduced in any form or by any electronic or mechanical means including information storage and retrieval systems, without permission in writing from the author. The only exception is by a reviewer, who may quote short excerpts in a review.

Although the author and publisher have made every effort to ensure that the information in this book was correct at press time, the author and publisher do not assume and hereby disclaim any liability to any party for any loss, damage, or disruption caused by errors or omissions, whether such errors or omissions result from negligence, accident, or any other cause.

This publication is designed to provide accurate and authoritative information with regard to the subject matter covered. It is sold with the understanding that the publisher is not engaged in rendering professional services. If legal advice or other expert assistance is required, the services of a competent professional should be sought.

The fact that an organization or website is referred to in this work as a citation and/or a potential source of further information does not mean that the author or the publisher endorses the information the organization or website may provide or recommendations it may make.

Please remember that Internet websites listed in this work may have changed or disappeared between when this work was written and when it is read.

To You,

Thank you!

Contents

Introduction 1

Chapter 1: Understanding Work-Life Balance 4
    Defining Work-Life Balance 4
    Importance of Work-Life Balance in Modern Times 7

Chapter 2: Remote Work Realities 10
    Transitioning to Remote Work 10
    Overcoming Remote Work Challenges 13

Chapter 3: Managing Stress Effectively 16
    Identifying Sources of Stress 16
    Techniques for Stress Reduction 19

Chapter 4: Setting Boundaries in a Blurred World 22
    Establishing Work and Personal Boundaries 22
    Communicating Boundaries Effectively 25

Chapter 5: Adapting to New Work Environments 29
    Embracing Hybrid Work Models 29
    Navigating Changes in Office Dynamics 32

Chapter 6: Enhancing Productivity and Well-being 35
    Strategies for Enhancing Productivity 35
    Incorporating Well-being Practices 38

Chapter 7: Technology and Balance 42
    Leveraging Technology for Balance 42
    Avoiding Technology Burnout 45

Chapter 8: Supporting Working Parents 49
    Challenges Faced by Working Parents 49
    Support Systems and Solutions for Parents 52

Chapter 9: Strategies for Entrepreneurs 56
    Balance Tips for Entrepreneurs 56
    Maintaining Passion Without Burnout 59

Chapter 10: Leadership and Management Approaches 62
    Leadership Strategies for Team Balance 62
    Implementing Employee Supportive Policies 65

Chapter 11: HR's Role in Work-Life Harmony 69
    Developing HR Policies for Balance 69
    Encouraging Organizational Culture Change 72

Chapter 12: Personal Growth and Self-Care 76
    Prioritizing Personal Growth 76
    Self-Care Practices for Long-Term Balance 79

Conclusion 80

Appendix A: Resources and Further Reading 83
    Books 83
    Articles 84
    Podcasts 84
    Websites and Online Resources 84
    Well-being Apps 84

Introduction

In today's fast-paced world, the lines between our professional and personal lives have become increasingly blurred. As we navigate this landscape, finding a harmonious balance between work and life has become more challenging, yet more critical, than ever. The need for a sophisticated understanding of work-life balance is underscored by the new realities brought about by the pandemic, which have fundamentally changed how we perceive work and home.

This book is crafted for a diverse array of readers—remote workers, entrepreneurs, working parents, managers, HR professionals, and anyone striving for better balance in their lives. Whether you're looking to regain control after experiencing burnout or simply seeking to maintain a healthy equilibrium in a demanding job, the strategies and insights shared here aim to empower you. Our intention is not just to offer solutions, but to provide a comprehensive framework that helps you to adapt to the continuously evolving work environment, reducing stress, and enhancing well-being.

The journey to achieving work-life balance often begins with understanding what it truly means. For some, it might be about spending more quality time with family, while for others, it could entail finding time for personal growth and hobbies. Regardless of one's priorities, a common thread remains: the pursuit of a more meaningful and less stressful life.

As you delve into this book, you'll find that each chapter is designed to address specific aspects of work-life balance. The first few sections provide insight into the fundamental concepts and importance of this balance, especially in our modern age. From the challenges of remote work to effective stress management, each chapter offers practical approaches to tackle these issues head-on.

The shift towards remote and hybrid work models has opened up new avenues for flexibility but also introduced unique challenges. Exploring ways to overcome these difficulties and the art of setting clear boundaries can greatly enhance one's ability to thrive in such environments. The need to clearly delineate work from personal time is no longer a luxury but a necessity to maintain mental health and productivity.

In an era where technology facilitates constant connectivity, using it wisely to maintain balance is crucial. While technology can be leveraged to support productivity, it also poses the risk of burnout if not carefully managed. Techniques for utilizing technology to our advantage while avoiding its pitfalls are therefore vital in crafting a balanced lifestyle.

Working parents, too, face a unique set of challenges that require specific considerations and support systems. Similarly, entrepreneurs must balance their passion for their ventures with personal life to prevent burnout. This book delves into strategies and support mechanisms for these groups, acknowledging the diverse struggles and triumphs they experience.

Leadership and managerial roles come with their own set of responsibilities in fostering a balanced workplace culture. Leaders are in a unique position to implement policies that prioritize balance and support their teams effectively. By encouraging an organizational culture that values employee well-being, companies can achieve greater overall satisfaction and productivity.

Likewise, HR professionals play a pivotal role in developing policies that enhance work-life harmony, advocating for changes that support individual and collective growth. Through progressive HR strategies, organizations can initiate cultural shifts that prioritize flexibility, support, and balance.

Personal growth and self-care emerge as crucial elements in sustaining a work-life balance over the long haul. Investing in oneself not only benefits the individual but also enhances their ability to contribute positively to their environment. As readers journey through these discussions, they will encounter actionable self-care practices that fortify their efforts towards achieving a fulfilling balance.

This book is structured to guide you through these various topics methodically, providing both broad perspectives and detailed strategies. The design is intentional, ensuring each chapter seamlessly builds upon the last, offering insights that are relevant to the multiple facets of your personal and professional life.

Our goal is to equip you with a toolkit of strategies and insights that you can adapt to suit your unique circumstances. Just as each person's definition of balance is different, so too are the paths to achieving it. By the time you reach the conclusion, our hope is that you'll not only be inspired but also armed with practical methods to start, or continue, your journey towards a balanced life.

The post-pandemic world demands resilience, adaptability, and a greater emphasis on mental and emotional well-being. This book provides both a compass and a map for navigating these unprecedented times. By integrating the wisdom of various thought leaders and weaving in practical advice, our exploration seeks to empower you to create and sustain the life you envision, one that's balanced and enriched in every possible way.

Chapter 1:
Understanding Work-Life Balance

Today's fast-paced, interconnected world has redefined work-life balance as more than just a buzzword; it's become a critical component of modern professional life. Rarely are the lines between work responsibilities and personal life as distinct as they once were, challenging remote workers, entrepreneurs, and busy parents alike to find equilibrium. Achieving that balance is not about distributing equal hours to work and leisure; rather, it's aligning both spheres in a way that fosters well-being and fulfillment. In essence, work-life balance is the ability to effectively manage one's workload without compromising personal spaces and relationships. While the digital age has introduced conveniences allowing us to work from virtually anywhere, it has also blurred the boundaries between professional duties and home life. Understanding these dynamics is essential, as neglecting balance can lead to stress and burnout, impacting productivity and mental health. As we delve deeper, recognizing the importance of work-life balance today sets the stage for developing robust strategies that accommodate the ever-evolving demands of post-pandemic lifestyles.

Defining Work-Life Balance

In today's fast-paced, always-connected world, work-life balance often feels like a pipe dream for many. But what exactly does work-life balance mean, especially in an era where personal and professional realms blur more than ever? At its core, work-life balance is about finding equilibrium between the demands of work and those of personal life. It's about being productive at work while also having time and energy for family, personal interests, and ultimately, oneself.

Work-life balance is not a one-size-fits-all proposition. Every individual's vision of balance is distinct, reflective of their personal priorities and professional obligations. For some, this may mean traditional work hours with strictly defined work and personal time. For others, it could involve more flexible schedules that accommodate personal interests or family needs. This diversity underscores that defining work-life balance is deeply personal, influenced by one's career stage, familial situations, and personal goals.

However, defining this balance also involves a philosophical shift in how we view time and productivity. It's about recognizing that time spent away from work is not a loss; instead, it contributes to overall well-being and enhances productivity at work. This perception shift is essential for both organizations and individuals aiming to foster environments conducive to sustainable work-life balance.

Underlying this balance is the understanding of boundaries. Boundaries are crucial as they define the limits we set to protect our time and energy. They help create a mental and physical separation between work and personal life, a distinction vital for maintaining mental health. Without clear boundaries, stress and burnout can quickly follow, impacting both personal happiness and professional performance.

There's also a communal aspect to work-life balance that often goes unnoticed. The support of one's family, friends, and colleagues plays a pivotal role here. When workplaces actively facilitate balance, perhaps by promoting flexible hours or focusing on employee well-being, they contribute significantly to an individual's pursuit of equilibrium. In turn, this can cultivate a supportive community where everyone feels encouraged to prioritize their personal needs alongside their professional duties.

The question then arises: how can we measure or recognize a balanced life? It's subjective, of course, varying widely among different people. For some, it might be the ability to enjoy uninterrupted family dinners or the freedom to pursue hobbies after work. For others, it might be as simple as feeling unstressed during a workweek or having the flexibility to attend a child's school event.

Technology, too, plays a dual role in the conversation about balance. On one hand, it allows unprecedented flexibility by enabling remote work, but on the other, it can tether us to work if not managed properly. Learning to leverage technology while setting boundaries with it becomes crucial in defining work-life balance.

As we navigate these concepts, it's important to remember that work-life balance is not about equal division of time between work and life. Rather, it's about recognizing the fluid nature of balance, accommodating life's ebb and flow, and realigning priorities as situations change. This flexibility is what sustains work-life harmony in the long run.

In crafting our own definitions of work-life balance, we align our lives in ways that resonate with our unique goals and values. It's an ongoing process of self-assessment, requiring honesty about what truly matters to us. By understanding and defining what balance means on an individual level, we're better equipped to seek it out and structure our lives accordingly.

Ultimately, a well-defined work-life balance is empowering. It's about taking control, making conscious choices about how we spend our time, and ensuring that both our personal and professional lives reflect our core values and aspirations. This definition becomes a guiding star, helping us navigate the complexities of modern living with greater ease and satisfaction.

Importance of Work-Life Balance in Modern Times

As we navigate the complexities of the modern workplace, the concept of work-life balance becomes increasingly significant. It's not just a buzzword but a critical aspect that influences our overall well-being and productivity. The evolving digital landscape and the aftermath of the global pandemic have redefined the boundaries between work and personal life, forcing us to rethink how we allocate our time and energy. This shift highlights the urgent need to understand and embrace work-life balance in ways that resonate with contemporary challenges and expectations.

Once upon a time, work and personal life were neatly segmented. You'd leave work at the office and return home to your personal pursuits without much overlap. Today, however, the lines between these domains are blurred, if not completely erased. The advent of technology allows constant connectivity, which can be both a boon and a bane. On one hand, it's easier for remote workers, entrepreneurs, and even working parents to stay updated and effective. On the other, this constant connection can lead to a relentless work cycle that envelops personal time, impeding relaxation and personal growth.

The importance of work-life balance extends beyond mere convenience. From a health perspective, chronic stress and the inability to disconnect from work can lead to serious physical and mental health issues, including burnout, anxiety, and depression. The World Health Organization has even classified burnout as an occupational phenomenon, characterized by feelings of energy depletion and reduced professional efficacy. Balancing work and life isn't merely about carving out leisure time—it's about reclaiming one's well-being and functionality in both personal and professional spaces.

For remote workers and entrepreneurs, work-life balance isn't just desirable—it's essential for maintaining creativity and motivation. When work invades personal life, creativity and enthusiasm tend to dwindle. A balanced approach, however, provides the mental space needed for innovation and sustained passion. It's a fertile ground for new ideas and solutions to flourish, which can lead to business success and personal fulfillment.

The conversation around work-life balance also reflects larger societal shifts. There's increased awareness and advocacy for mental health, self-care, and personal fulfillment. These trends emphasize the need for a holistic approach to work and life, focusing on how they interact and support each other. Individuals and organizations are encouraged to re-evaluate their priorities and strategies, recognizing that happiness and productivity can coexist and enhance one another.

Furthermore, the modern emphasis on work-life balance has prompted changes at organizational levels. Companies are starting to realize that supporting their employees' work-life balance is not just altruistic but also beneficial to the organization's success. Happy, balanced employees are often more productive, engaged, and less likely to leave the company. Policies that support flexible working conditions, mental health days, and personal growth opportunities are becoming more prevalent, reflecting a broader cultural shift toward employee-centric work environments.

Managers and HR professionals play a pivotal role in fostering this balance. By creating supportive policies and encouraging a culture that values balance, they help build an environment where employees can thrive. This approach not only enhances employee satisfaction but also builds a loyal and resilient workforce. Leaders are learning that promoting a work-life balance is integral to a successful and sustainable business model.

Harmony at Hand

For working parents, juggling the demands of work and family life can be especially challenging. The need for work-life balance in this context takes on a critical, existential dimension. Without it, parents risk burnout and strained relationships with their children and partners. Recognizing this, many companies are offering supportive structures like parental leave and flexible work hours, demonstrating a commitment to the well-being of working parents and their families.

Achieving work-life balance in today's world means mastering boundary-setting while remaining adaptable. It's about knowing when to unplug and when to engage, a skill crucial in maintaining personal well-being. As we adapt to new work environments, learning how to balance becomes an integral part of thriving, both in work and in life. Work-life balance is no longer an aspirational goal—it is a necessity for sustainable living in modern times.

In conclusion, the importance of work-life balance is unmistakable in our modern world. It is a linchpin that supports physical health, mental well-being, creativity, and overall quality of life. The onus lies on individuals, leaders, and companies to recognize this and take proactive steps to integrate balance into everyday life. By doing so, we not only enhance our own lives but also contribute positively to the organizations and communities we are part of, creating a harmonious and productive future for all. As we strive to adapt to the evolving demands of work and life, balancing these aspects remains crucial to our success and happiness in the modern era.

Chapter 2:
Remote Work Realities

As we delve into the essence of remote work, we find ourselves navigating a landscape that offers both freedom and complexity. The transition from traditional office settings to remote environments has rewritten the script for how individuals and teams operate. While the flexibility to work from any location can lead to higher autonomy and satisfaction, this new reality also presents challenges such as isolation, blurred work-life boundaries, and a continuous struggle to maintain effective communication and collaboration. Over time, remote work calls for a recalibration of our routines and mindsets, pushing us to develop new strategies to remain connected yet balanced in our professional and personal endeavors. The realities of this evolving work model compel us to refine our skills, adapt our technologies, and reorder our priorities to achieve sustainable success in both career and life.

Transitioning to Remote Work

The shift to remote work has been one of the most profound transformations in the professional landscape in recent years. The traditional office setting is being redefined, offering both unprecedented opportunities and formidable challenges. As the world adapts to this new norm, understanding the nuances of transitioning effectively becomes crucial.

For many, remote work presents a welcome change: no more long commutes, greater flexibility, and the comfort of home. However, this transition requires more than just a change in location; it's a shift in mindset. Traditional office routines and boundaries blur when your living space doubles as your workspace. Individuals must reevaluate their time management strategies, develop new routines, and cultivate an environment conducive to productivity.

Creating a distinct workspace at home is the first step towards ensuring focus and efficiency. This space, ideally separate from areas of leisure and rest, acts as a physical boundary that delineates work from personal life. It doesn't need to be elaborate; even a small dedicated corner with a chair and desk can instill a sense of purpose and routine.

Beyond the physical setup, the technological shift is another critical aspect of transitioning to remote work. High-speed internet, reliable hardware, and effective software tools are non-negotiables for maintaining productivity and connectivity. The current digital era offers numerous tools designed to mimic in-person office interactions, ensuring teams remain cohesive despite physical distances. It's not just about being equipped; it's about utilizing these technologies to their full potential to forge connections and collaboration.

Communication, always a linchpin in professional success, takes on a new form in a remote setting. Frequent, clear communication becomes even more critical to address potential misunderstandings and misalignments. Video calls, instant messaging, and project management platforms fill the void left by face-to-face interactions. Establishing regular check-ins and feedback loops helps maintain alignment on goals and tasks, preventing anyone from feeling isolated.

Adapting to remote work involves a psychological adjustment too. The home, traditionally a sanctuary from work stresses, now includes them. It becomes imperative to mentally 'switch off' and maintain a work-life balance. Establishing a consistent start and end time to each workday, taking regular breaks, and respecting personal time are essential practices. Just because your office is at home doesn't mean you're available round the clock.

Remote work also invites greater autonomy and responsibility. Employers trust their teams to manage their tasks effectively without constant supervision. This autonomy can be empowering, providing opportunities for innovation and creativity. However, with greater freedom comes the need for self-discipline. Time management skills are more crucial than ever, with tools like calendars, timers, and to-do lists becoming invaluable assets.

For managers, leading a remote team demands a shift in focus from micromanaging to fostering trust and empowerment. Performance metrics shift from hours logged to quality of output and meeting objectives. Effective leadership in a remote environment involves being supportive, accessible, and adaptable to the varied circumstances of team members. Recognizing achievements and providing constructive feedback are vital in maintaining morale and motivation when physical celebrations and gatherings aren't feasible.

Transitioning to remote work impacts not just the individual, but families too. Households might need to adapt to having more than one person working or studying from home. This shift can strain relationships and increase stress. Clear communication with family members about work hours and spaces can alleviate some of these pressures, reinforcing both work and familial harmony.

For working parents, the transition can be particularly challenging. Balancing work tasks with parenting duties requires creative solutions and, often, external support. Having a clear schedule and setting boundaries with employers regarding non-negotiable family times helps in managing expectations and reducing stress.

The transition to remote work is ongoing, with continuous learning and adaptation. Techniques and strategies will evolve as technology advances and as organizations and individuals become more accustomed to the dynamic work environment. Those on this journey must remain flexible and open to change, ready to embrace the inevitable shifts in working paradigms.

Ultimately, successful remote work transition comes down to balance—between work and life, connection and solitude, structure and flexibility. While the path may be complex, the potential rewards in terms of enhanced well-being, efficiency, and satisfaction are profound. For those willing to embrace this new reality with open minds and resilient spirits, the possibilities are limitless.

Overcoming Remote Work Challenges

Remote work has transformed the way we engage with our daily tasks, offering flexibility and autonomy, but it's not without its hurdles. It's important to recognize these challenges as opportunities for growth. Addressing remote work challenges is essential for achieving work-life balance, maintaining productivity, and ensuring long-term satisfaction. The first step is understanding common difficulties faced by remote workers, from feelings of isolation to the strain of balancing home and work life in the same space.

One of the most prominent challenges is the struggle with isolation. Many workers miss the spontaneous interactions and camaraderie of a traditional office setting, which can result in a sense of loneliness or disconnect. To overcome this, remote workers can create a virtual community. Companies can facilitate regular team check-ins or virtual coffee breaks, encouraging social interactions that foster a sense of belonging. Additionally, participating in local coworking spaces, when feasible, can help bridge the gap between remote work and social interaction.

Managing time effectively in a remote work setup is another hurdle. Without the clear boundaries of an office environment, workers often find themselves overextending their work hours, leading to burnout. One effective strategy is adopting a structured schedule. Utilize tools like digital calendars or time-blocking techniques to delineate work hours clearly. Incorporating breaks and setting a definitive end to the workday fosters a balanced lifestyle. It's equally important to communicate these boundaries with family members or roommates to minimize disruptions and maintain focus during work hours.

Distractions are inevitable when working from home. Whether it's household chores, children seeking attention, or the allure of personal devices, staying productive can be tough. To combat this, creating a designated workspace is crucial. This doesn't have to be a separate room but should be an area associated solely with work. Personalize it to what inspires concentration and minimizes interruptions. Furthermore, using productivity apps like focus timers or task management tools can help maintain momentum throughout the day, keeping distractions at bay.

Technology, while a boon, can also be a bane. Constant connectivity can blur lines between personal and professional time, compounding work stress. One way to manage this is through digital detox strategies during off-hours. Encourage shutting down work devices after work hours and being mindful of notifications. Companies can support this by respecting employees' non-work hours and promoting a culture where "always connected" is not the norm.

Security concerns are another layer of complexity in remote work. Protecting sensitive information and ensuring secure connections are vital. Employing virtual private networks (VPNs), secure Wi-Fi connections, and regularly updating software to combat potential cyber threats create a safer digital environment. Additionally, remote workers should be educated on best cybersecurity practices to mitigate risks.

The lack of a clear career development path is a significant concern for many remote workers. Without face-to-face interactions, potential growth within a company may seem ambiguous. Organizations can address this by establishing transparent career pathways, actively involving remote workers in training opportunities, mentorship programs, and regular performance reviews. Encouraging continued learning and personal development helps employees feel valued and pushes their professional boundaries.

Lastly, emphasizing mental health and well-being cannot be overstated. Remote workers often overlook the importance of taking care of their mental health due to blurred boundaries and work intensification. Incorporating wellness practices such as regular exercise, meditation, or any form of self-care into daily routines can provide grounding and rejuvenate the mind and body. Employers should offer support through wellness resources, mental health days, or access to counseling services.

Overcoming remote work challenges demands a proactive approach from individuals and organizations alike. By fostering communication, implementing structured schedules, utilizing technology wisely, and prioritizing mental health, remote workers can thrive. These solutions not only enhance productivity but also nurture a balanced work-life synergy, ultimately leading to a more fulfilling remote work experience.

Chapter 3:
Managing Stress Effectively

Managing stress effectively is essential in today's fast-paced work environment, especially for remote workers, entrepreneurs, and anyone balancing a myriad of commitments. Stress doesn't just stem from workloads or deadlines, but often lurks in the unresolved conflicts between our professional responsibilities and personal aspirations. Recognizing these triggers is the first step toward conquering them. A proactive approach involves integrating simple yet meaningful techniques into daily routines, such as mindfulness practices and strategic breaks, which can dramatically improve our resilience. Embracing stress management isn't a one-size-fits-all journey; it's a personalized strategy that evolves as your needs change. By fostering a culture where stress is acknowledged and addressed, we cultivate not only a healthier mindset but also more productive environments both at home and in the workplace.

Identifying Sources of Stress

As we delve deeper into managing stress effectively, understanding what exactly triggers our stress is crucial. Pinpointing stressors isn't just an exercise in self-awareness; it's a vital step toward meaningful change. Our lives, especially post-pandemic, are more intertwined with technology, punctuated by constant pings and notifications that demand immediate attention. The digital landscape, while filled with conveniences, can often serve as a breeding ground for stress.

For remote workers and entrepreneurs, the lines between professional and personal time have blurred considerably. This lack of clear boundaries is a significant stress source. Tasks that never seemed urgent now make it harder to switch off. Accessibility almost always leads to a sense of perpetual availability. Is it any wonder that burnout rates have escalated? Identifying these patterns is the first step towards reclaiming our time and mental peace.

Working parents are not immune to stress, as the expectations stack up both at work and home. Juggling work tasks while trying to nurture and care for young minds is daunting. When school closures or lack of childcare options come into play, stress levels can skyrocket. It's not just about time management, it's about being emotionally present in both spheres without feeling stretched too thin.

Entrepreneurs, with their unrelenting drive and high stakes, face unique stressors. The pressure to succeed, manage finances, and maintain passion without succumbing to exhaustion can be overwhelming. Passion projects can easily transform into stress-inducing burdens if not carefully managed. Recognizing these early signs helps in redirecting energy back into healthy, productive pathways.

Then there's the realm of corporate managers and HR professionals who are responsible for overseeing not just their own work-life balance but also advocating for their teams. The expectation to be the anchor of stability and support in tumultuous times is daunting. Stress can manifest in various ways, from feeling inadequately supported by upper management to dealing with the repercussions of a company's shifting policies.

Beyond the individual responsibilities and roles, overarching themes contribute to stress. Time management appears as an inevitable factor. It's a universal trigger, impacting everyone from working parents to managers. Feeling a lack of time to accomplish tasks weighs heavily, exacerbating stress and fostering feelings of inadequacy.

Technology, albeit a boon, is another double-edged sword. While it enables remote working, it can drive people to be online continuously. Smartphones, computers, and emails might be essential, but they disrupt personal time, causing digital fatigue. The trick is to balance between benefitting from technological advances and recognizing when they tip into stress-inducing territories.

Environment plays a significant role in stress identification. A cluttered space can mirror a cluttered mind. Remote work has thrust many into makeshift home offices where the environment isn't always conducive to productivity. This leads to irritation, decreased morale, and stress. Thoughtful adjustment of one's environment can alleviate these issues considerably.

Adapting to these stressors means recognizing the distinct cultures and dynamics within different workplaces, whether that's a corporate office adjusting to hybrid work models or an at-home workspace. Each environment presents unique challenges that can fuel stress. Navigating these involves understanding the dynamics in play and the specific stressors they generate.

Moreover, individual differences shouldn't be overlooked. Personality types significantly influence how stress is perceived and handled. What causes significant stress for one person might be a minor irritation for another. This variance means customized strategies are paramount when addressing stressors. Introverts may struggle with constant Zoom meetings, while extroverts might dread the isolation remote work can promote.

Stress is not entirely negative; it can signal when we're stretching beyond limits, serving as a reminder to reassess priorities and focus. By proactively identifying stress sources, individuals can develop strategies not only to cope but to thrive in a rapidly evolving environment. Understanding these stressors places us in a stronger position to cultivate genuine work-life balance.

Techniques for Stress Reduction

In today's fast-paced and often unpredictable world, stress reduction has become more than just a luxury; it's a necessity. As we navigate evolving work environments and juggle diverse roles, understanding stress-reduction techniques is crucial. Various effective methods can help alleviate the pressures we face daily.

One of the most accessible techniques is practicing mindfulness. This doesn't mean you need to meditate for hours on end. Mindfulness can simply involve paying attention to the present moment without judgment. When you're overwhelmed, try focusing on your breathing for a few minutes. Inhale deeply, hold for a moment, and then exhale slowly. This practice helps ground your thoughts, leading to a sense of calm and clarity.

Exercise is another powerful tool for stress reduction. Regular physical activity releases endorphins, chemicals in the brain that act as natural painkillers and mood elevators. Whether you prefer a morning jog, a session of yoga, or an evening walk, incorporating movement into your routine can significantly improve your stress levels. It's important to choose activities you enjoy because you're more likely to stick with them.

Social connections also play a pivotal role in reducing stress. Engaging with friends, family, or colleagues allows you to process your feelings and gain new perspectives. Virtual meet-ups, phone calls, or even brief text exchanges can help strengthen these bonds. It's not about having a large network but rather cultivating a few strong, meaningful relationships.

Time management practices can significantly alleviate stress, especially for those balancing multiple responsibilities. Start by prioritizing tasks and set realistic goals for each day. Consider using techniques like the Pomodoro Technique, where you work for 25 minutes followed by a 5-minute break. This method helps maintain focus and reduces burnout, making your workload feel more manageable.

Creating a balanced environment also aids in stress management. Start by de-cluttering your workspace to reduce distractions. A tidy, organized space can promote efficiency and alleviate anxiety. Additionally, consider using ambient sounds or music to create a relaxing atmosphere that supports concentration and creativity.

At times, stress can stem from an overfilled schedule. Learning to say 'no' is essential. It's important to recognize your limits and not overcommit. Prioritize tasks and commitments that align with your goals and values. By doing so, you free up time for activities that truly matter and bring joy into your life.

Incorporating relaxation techniques into your daily routine is another effective way to manage stress. Methods such as progressive muscle relaxation, where you systematically tense and release different muscle groups, can reduce physical tension and mental stress. Guided imagery, on the other hand, invites you to visualize calming scenes or experiences, aiding relaxation and peace of mind.

Journaling is a reflective practice that can provide stress relief. Writing about your thoughts and feelings can help process emotions and identify stressors. Setting aside a few minutes each day to jot down your reflections can lead to insights and a greater understanding of what triggers stress and how best to manage it.

Nutrition also plays a crucial role in stress management. Consuming a balanced diet rich in whole foods, like fruits, vegetables, and lean proteins, supports brain health and enhances mood stability. Stay hydrated and moderate caffeine intake, as it can increase anxiety if consumed excessively.

Sleep cannot be overlooked when discussing stress reduction strategies. Ensuring you get enough quality sleep each night allows your body and mind to recuperate. Establish a consistent sleep schedule by going to bed and waking up at the same time each day. Create a relaxing bedtime routine, eliminating screens at least an hour before sleep, to promote better rest.

Sometimes, professional support becomes necessary. Seeking therapy or counseling can provide valuable tools and strategies for managing stress effectively. Therapists can offer guidance tailored to your unique circumstances, helping you build resilience and cope with life's challenges.

Remember, stress reduction is an ongoing process that requires commitment and adaptation. What works today might not be as effective tomorrow, so remain open to experimenting with different techniques and adjusting them as needed. The path to a less stressful life involves embracing these practices to enhance your well-being and productivity.

Chapter 4:
Setting Boundaries in a Blurred World

In today's ever-connected world, finding the balance between work and personal life feels more challenging than ever. With digital devices and remote work blurring the lines between job duties and personal time, setting boundaries becomes crucial for maintaining both productivity and well-being. Imagine trying to focus on a project while household responsibilities demand attention; the ability to establish clear separations becomes a lifeline. Workers and leaders alike must skillfully balance flexibility with firmness, ensuring they aren't always on call but still accessible. This delicate dance involves not just self-discipline but also effective communication with colleagues, managers, and family members. Articulating personal boundaries helps manage expectations and fosters mutual respect, creating an environment where both work and life can coexist harmoniously. As we navigate this blurred world, setting these lines isn't just about finding balance—it's about reclaiming control and fostering a space where both aspects of our lives can thrive.

Establishing Work and Personal Boundaries

In today's interconnected world, where the lines between our professional and personal lives have become increasingly blurred, establishing boundaries is more crucial than ever. The convenience of remote work and digital advancements brings along challenges, particularly the challenge of maintaining distinct spaces for our work and personal lives. This shift towards a borderless work environment requires conscious effort to draw the lines that prevent our work from spilling over into our personal time.

Initially, it may feel liberating to check emails at odd hours or take personal calls during work meetings, but this flexibility can quickly lead to burnout if not managed properly. When work and personal tasks intermingle throughout the day, it can become overwhelming and difficult to switch off. Establishing boundaries is not just about protecting your time; it's about preserving your mental well-being.

Begin by identifying what truly matters in both spheres of your life. What are the core values and priorities driving your work? Which personal activities and relationships genuinely enrich your life? By understanding these priorities, you create a foundation upon which to build solid boundaries. It's essential to reconcile these priorities with your responsibilities, since they will guide you in setting limits that reflect both your professional goals and personal needs.

Physical boundaries play a critical role in this process. Even in a remote work setting, where geographical boundaries are nonexistent, it's important to designate specific spaces for different activities. If possible, allocate a particular area in your home as your workspace and reserve other areas for personal and family activities. This physical segregation can enhance focus during work hours and relaxation when you're off the clock.

Time boundaries are equally vital. Defining work hours and sticking to them is a simple yet effective method to ensure that neither sphere dominates the other. Set clear start and stop times for your workday and ensure others are aware of them. During work hours, dedicate your attention fully to professional tasks; likewise, once the workday ends, resist the urge to engage in work-related activities.

Reflect on your digital habits, as they are often responsible for blurring these boundaries. The temptation to remain constantly available can be irresistible with smartphones, tablets, and laptops within arms' reach. Protect your personal time by setting boundaries for email and message notifications after work hours. Use technology to your advantage, such as scheduling focus time on your calendar or setting 'do not disturb' modes on devices.

Involve others in your boundary-setting efforts, particularly those who influence your daily routines. Communicate your boundaries clearly with colleagues, clients, and family members. Honest and open discussions about your availability and priorities will foster mutual respect and understanding. Encourage them to honor your boundaries by doing the same for them, creating a work culture that values and respects personal time.

Moreover, be prepared to face challenges along the way. Establishing boundaries will often test your resolve, especially when faced with urgent work tasks or personal obligations. Remember that the initial discomfort or resistance from others will gradually give way to respect as they witness the positive impact it has on your productivity and well-being. A well-articulated boundary can strengthen relationships across the board, as it underlines a commitment to being present in each moment.

Boundaries are not static; they require regular reassessment and adjustments to remain effective. As you or your life circumstances change, so too should your boundaries. Whether it's a change in job responsibilities or a new personal commitment, adapt your boundaries to reflect these shifts. Periodic reflection on what's working and what's not will help in maintaining healthy equilibrium between your work and personal life.

Many individuals also find it helpful to engage in rituals or habits to demarcate working and personal times. Consider developing a routine that signifies the beginning and end of your workday, such as a short walk or a specific playlist. Such practices will support the mental transition between roles, signaling the brain to switch gears efficiently.

By placing importance on crafting these boundaries, we not only protect our time but also cultivate an environment where we can thrive both professionally and personally. This harmonious balance empowers us to perform at our best and invest wholeheartedly in both realms. In building and respecting these boundaries, we contribute not just to our own well-being but also create a ripple effect that promotes a culture of balance and respect in our workplaces and homes.

Embrace the opportunity to lead by example. When you uphold strong boundaries, you send a clear message about valuing self-care and balance, encouraging others to seek equilibrium in their lives too. In doing so, you become a catalyst for fostering healthier work environments and more fulfilling personal spaces.

Communicating Boundaries Effectively

In today's interconnected world, the lines between work and personal life often blur. Communicating boundaries effectively becomes crucial in maintaining a balance that nurtures both our professional aspirations and personal well-being. This task is not merely about stating preferences but involves a deliberate and thoughtful engagement with others to foster mutual understanding and respect.

One might think of boundaries as invisible lines drawn to protect one's time and energy. Yet, communicating them can often feel like navigating a complex maze. It's essential to recognize that boundary-setting is an art, nuanced and subtle, demanding both precision and empathy. The aim is to convey your needs without alienating or offending others, whether they're colleagues, supervisors, or even family members.

Let's start with the fundamentals. Before you can communicate boundaries, you must clearly identify what they are. Spend time introspecting your limits—what times you're willing to allocate for work-related calls, when you prefer not to be disturbed for personal reflection or family time, and how you envision your ideal work-life scenario. Clarity with yourself paves the way for clarity with others.

Once internal clarity is achieved, the next step is external communication. Initiate conversations where boundaries naturally fit the context. Maybe it's as simple as setting DO NOT DISTURB times on your calendar, or as complex as a dialogue with your supervisor about your roles and responsibilities. Key here is to present your boundaries in a way that underscores a win-win for all involved. When others see the benefits, they're more likely to support your boundary settings.

Language plays a pivotal role in communicating boundaries. It's not just about what you say but how you say it. Using "I" statements can help in expressing personal needs without sounding accusatory. Instead of saying, "You should not call after 6 PM," you might say, "I work best when I can unwind after 6 PM without interruptions." Such phrasing helps in framing the boundary as a supportive measure for productivity and mental health rather than a barrier to collaboration.

Empathy acts as a cornerstone in this process. Understand that people around you may have differing priorities and pressures. By showing empathy and flexibility, you foster an environment where mutual respect for boundaries thrives. Sometimes, this means being open to temporary boundary adjustments during critical project deadlines or personal emergencies.

Technology, while often complicit in blurring lines, can also serve as a powerful ally in boundary enforcement. Tools like calendar apps can help schedule uninterrupted work blocks, while communication platforms offer status indicators to signal availability. By harnessing technology's potential, you can tactfully reinforce your boundaries without requiring constant verbal reminders.

Harmony at Hand

Challenges abound, and the fear of negative repercussions can inhibit boundary communication. It's natural to worry about how a colleague or manager might perceive your needs. However, addressing such apprehensions head-on is vital. Engaging in open dialogues can reveal surprising support and even encourage others to establish their own boundaries. Often, boundary-setting can catalyze a broader cultural shift towards respect and balance.

Recognize that some resistance may arise, and that's okay. Not everyone will embrace your boundaries immediately. Maintain consistency in your boundaries and keep communication channels open. Express appreciation for others' understanding and be willing to listen to their needs as well. This creates a cycle of mutual respect and shared responsibility in maintaining an environment conducive to productivity and well-being.

Sometimes it helps to ally with others who share similar boundary challenges. Whether it's a colleague, a mentor, or a peer group, having allies can bolster your confidence and provide support. Sharing experiences and strategies for boundary communication strengthens resolve and builds community around mutual goals of balance and mental wellness.

Let's not forget the importance of following up. Setting a boundary is not a single event but a continuous process. Check-in with yourself and, if appropriate, with those affected by your boundaries. Are they being respected? Are adjustments needed? Regularly revisiting these questions ensures that your boundaries remain relevant and effective, adapting to new circumstances as needed.

As we navigate this blurred world, remember that boundaries need not be rigid. They should be adaptable, open to evolution as personal and professional landscapes shift. Flexibility does not mean compromise on core needs but allows for a dynamic balance that accommodates growth and change. Embracing this mindset equips you with resilience, preparing you to handle the unexpected twists and turns life presents.

In conclusion, effectively communicating boundaries is an ongoing dialogue—an art that blends clarity, empathy, and adaptability. As you refine this skill, you not only protect your well-being but also contribute to a healthier, more balanced environment for everyone involved. Empowered by these strategies, we can embrace the blurred lines of our modern world, not as constraints but as opportunities for empathetic connection and harmonious coexistence.

Chapter 5:
Adapting to New Work Environments

In today's rapidly changing landscape, adapting to new work environments is essential for thriving both professionally and personally. As the dust settles from the global shift induced by the pandemic, workers and organizations are embracing hybrid work models that cater to diverse needs. This evolution calls for greater flexibility, the ability to navigate office dynamics with finesse, and an open mind to change. Workers are now crafting personalized approaches that blend the physical and virtual realms, where a traditional nine-to-five doesn't always apply. This transition isn't always smooth, but it presents an opportunity to redefine our workspaces, making them conducive to greater balance and productivity. By staying adaptable, individuals and teams can leverage these changes to foster collaboration, maintain focus, and support well-being in a world where work and life interlace more than ever before.

Embracing Hybrid Work Models

The concept of hybrid work models has emerged as a significant player in the landscape of modern work environments. This evolution is driven by the necessity to accommodate diverse work preferences while maintaining productivity and employee satisfaction. In this transitional phase, businesses are discovering the compelling benefits of blending remote and in-office work, creating a dynamic that caters to the varied needs of employees across different roles and industries.

Hybrid models offer a flexible approach, allowing for customization based on individual preferences, job responsibilities, and company culture. For remote workers, this flexibility can feel like a breath of fresh air. It recognizes the reality that some tasks can be more effectively performed without the distractions of a busy office, enhancing focus and productivity. Yet, there's also a social and collaborative element to work that can't be entirely replicated through digital communication.

For entrepreneurs, hybrid models can provide a strategic advantage. By mixing in-person and remote work, business owners have the potential to tap into a global talent pool without the overhead costs associated with maintaining a fully staffed office space. Such a model can enable startups to grow and innovate without being tied down by geographical limitations.

Working parents find hybrid work arrangements particularly beneficial. The ability to work from home part of the week can facilitate better coordination of family responsibilities, reducing the parental juggling act between professional obligations and family life. This setup can lessen the stress often associated with balancing these roles, thereby enhancing satisfaction and productivity both at work and at home.

Managers play an essential role in the transition to hybrid work models. They must adapt their strategies to manage teams that don't always share the same physical space. This requires new tools and techniques for communication and collaboration to ensure everyone feels included and informed. Effective management in a hybrid environment also involves trusting employees to get their work done without constant supervision, focusing instead on outcomes rather than physical presence.

HR professionals face unique challenges and opportunities with hybrid work models. Developing policies that recognize the nuances of hybrid work is crucial. These policies should address issues like communication norms, compensation, and performance metrics while ensuring equity and consistency. HR's proactive role in training employees and fostering an organizational culture that embraces hybrid models can bridge gaps and foster harmony.

For individuals overcoming burnout, hybrid models can present a viable path to recovery. The mix of remote work can offer the time and space needed to recuperate, while periodic office interactions can slowly reintegrate them into the social aspects of work in a manageable way. This gradual return can help ease stress and diminish feelings of isolation.

It's important to recognize that hybrid work isn't a one-size-fits-all solution. Companies must frequently assess and adjust these models to meet their specific needs and the evolving expectations of their workforce. Open communication lines between employers and employees can help in crafting a system that works for everyone.

While hybrid work models aren't without their challenges, they represent a relationship shift between employers and employees that prioritizes balance, well-being, and flexibility. By strategically embracing these models, organizations can potentially boost innovation, motivation, and loyalty, driving them toward a more sustainable future.

The hybrid work model exemplifies the future of work itself: adaptable, inclusive, and ready to meet the demands of a changing world. With a focus on creating an environment that empowers employees to perform at their best, companies can pave the way for a new era of work-life harmony, tailor-made for the post-pandemic world.

Navigating Changes in Office Dynamics

As organizations worldwide adapt to new work models, the traditional office dynamic has evolved significantly. These shifts have been accelerated by the global shift towards remote and hybrid work, prompting profound changes in workplace interactions and processes. Understanding how to navigate these changes is crucial for maintaining harmony and productivity in the organizational environment.

The office no longer resembles the clearly divided space of old. Physical workspaces have evolved, and the boundaries between home and office blur with each passing day. As teams grapple with these transformations, new dynamics in communication and collaboration emerge, requiring both employers and employees to embrace a culture of adaptability and innovation.

One of the primary challenges is fostering collaboration in a mixed environment where some team members work remotely while others are physically present. This hybrid setup requires a concerted effort to ensure all employees remain engaged and connected. People must learn to navigate different communication tools seamlessly, transitioning from spontaneous in-person chats to structured virtual meetings. The key is to balance these interactions to maintain a cohesive team spirit.

In addition to transforming how employees collaborate, the role of managers has evolved dramatically. A shift has occurred from overseeing daily activities to providing support and guidance. Managers are now tasked with ensuring their teams are equipped to face new office dynamics, which includes offering flexible structures while maintaining accountability. Mentoring becomes pivotal, as employees navigate the challenges of working both independently and as part of a collective unit.

The office environment also significantly influences employee morale and well-being. As such, organizations must reconsider office layouts to suit hybrid work needs. Flexible workstations, quiet zones, and collaborative spaces cater to a diverse range of working preferences, promoting productivity and well-being simultaneously. Moreover, providing options like hot desking can maximize the office's usability, catering to the varying needs of employees.

Embracing diversity and inclusion within these changing dynamics is more important than ever. An office that values diverse voices fosters a culture of respect and innovation, where everyone feels heard and appreciated. With varied perspectives, teams can approach problems more creatively, leading to richer, more effective solutions.

Building a strong organizational culture in this context extends beyond physical spaces. Employers must also focus on cultivating an environment of trust and transparency. This can be achieved by establishing clear communication channels and encouraging regular feedback. Listening to and addressing employee concerns proactively reaffirms their value, promoting higher levels of engagement and satisfaction.

Technology plays a significant role in navigating these new office dynamics. The implementation of robust digital platforms facilitates better team collaboration and communication, supporting both on-site and remote team members. Ensuring everyone has access to the same resources and information is critical for establishing an equitable work environment.

However, it's crucial not to rely too heavily on technology. While digital tools are essential for efficiency, they can also lead to burnout. Encouraging regular breaks and promoting a healthy work-life balance prevents technology from overshadowing personal interactions, which are equally important in building a connected, collaborative culture.

Training opportunities can empower staff to adapt to new office dynamics. Regular workshops and seminars on communication, stress management, and digital literacy help employees remain agile in the face of change. Encouraging lifelong learning fosters a culture of resilience and innovation, enabling individuals to thrive regardless of their work environment.

Moreover, as office dynamics evolve, it's important for leadership to recognize and celebrate milestones. Acknowledging team achievements, whether big or small, strengthens camaraderie and boosts morale. Recognition further helps in building a cohesive team, where every member feels like an integral part of the organization's journey.

Ultimately, navigating these changes is an ongoing journey, requiring commitment from both employees and organizations alike. By embracing flexibility, fostering open communication, and valuing diversity, everyone can thrive amidst the evolving office dynamics. The key is to remain open to change, viewing it not as a challenge, but as an opportunity for growth and innovation in our modern work environment.

Chapter 6:
Enhancing Productivity and Well-being

As we navigate the complexities of a post-pandemic work environment, enhancing both productivity and well-being becomes crucial for sustaining long-term success and satisfaction. By adopting mindful strategies, individuals can boost their productivity while ensuring their mental and physical health don't hang in the balance. At the heart of this transformation lies the commitment to developing habits that blend efficiency with self-care, allowing remote workers, entrepreneurs, and working parents to thrive without compromise. Techniques such as time-blocking, prioritizing tasks, and delegating effectively can lead to immense gains in productivity. Meanwhile, incorporating well-being practices like regular exercise, meditation, and setting aside time for personal interests fosters a holistic approach that sustains energy and motivation. This synergy between productive momentum and rejuvenating practices not only combats the risk of burnout but also cultivates a more fulfilling and harmonious work-life integration. By embracing these strategies, we open the door to a future where success and well-being walk hand in hand, building a resilient foundation for continued personal and professional growth.

Strategies for Enhancing Productivity

Boosting productivity isn't just about working longer or faster. It's about working smarter. Let's delve into some strategies that can fundamentally shift how we approach our work, whether from a home office, a bustling coffee shop, or a traditional workplace. It's time to rethink productivity not as a mechanical goal but as an intrinsic part of well-being.

Firstly, setting realistic goals is crucial. This doesn't mean lowering your standards but honing in on what's actually achievable within a given timeframe. Break down bigger projects into smaller, actionable tasks. This not only makes tasks less daunting but also keeps you motivated as you tick each one off your list. Try using the SMART criteria — specific, measurable, achievable, relevant, and time-bound — to create goals that keep you on track.

Time management is another vital component, and tools abound in this area. The Pomodoro Technique, for instance, involves focused work sessions followed by short breaks, which can enhance concentration and prevent burnout. This approach acknowledges that while our brains can be marvelously efficient, they also need rest to perform at their best.

Incorporating technology wisely can be a game-changer. There are countless apps and software solutions designed to boost productivity. Project management tools like Trello or Asana can help keep tasks organized and priorities clear. And it's not just about storing information but using automation to handle repetitive tasks. This technological assistance gives you more room to focus on activities that require deep thinking and creativity.

Distractions are the arch-nemesis of productivity. Identifying major distractions in your work environment and creating strategies to minimize them is pivotal. A cluttered workspace, for example, can be both a physical and mental distraction. Investing time into creating an organized, peaceful workspace can make a substantial difference.

Establishing a routine can also aid productivity. Our brains thrive on patterns and habit formation. By having a consistent start to your day — whether it's a morning walk, reading, or meditation — you signal your brain to switch into work mode. Over time, these rituals can help to decrease the mental load, allowing you to start your day with clarity and purpose.

Collaboration and communication play transformative roles in enhancing productivity, especially if you're working remotely or part of a team. Clear communication channels prevent misunderstandings and ensure everyone's on the same page. Regular check-ins, whether through video calls or regular messaging, can also boost team morale and accountability.

Let's not overlook the importance of well-being in the context of productivity. Exercise, proper nutrition, and adequate sleep are the fuels that power our productivity engines. Without these, even the most disciplined individual will struggle to maintain high levels of performance. Ensuring your well-being isn't a luxury; it's an essential element of productive work life.

Now, let's talk about the power of saying "no." It might sound counterproductive, but saying no to certain tasks can actually enhance productivity. It's about prioritizing tasks that align with your goals and delegating or declining those that don't. This doesn't mean shutting down every opportunity but rather thoughtfully considering how each aligns with your objectives and energy levels.

Taking regular breaks is non-negotiable. Despite the urge to power through, our minds are not designed to function in continuous high-output mode. Short pauses and longer breaks alike rejuvenate us, prevent fatigue, and often result in the "aha" moments that push projects forward.

Finally, continuous reflection and adaptability are key. Regularly reviewing what strategies are and aren't working allows us to recalibrate. Successful productivity isn't static; it evolves as our circumstances and understandings do. Stay open to new tools and methods that might adjust your productivity style to suit your current context.

As you integrate these strategies, remember, productivity is deeply personal. Not every method will work for everyone, but with experimentation and commitment, you'll discover a rhythm that enhances both your productivity and well-being.

Incorporating Well-being Practices

In an era where the lines between professional and personal life blur more by the day, incorporating well-being practices into our daily routines is no longer just a luxury—it's a necessity. For remote workers, entrepreneurs, and working parents, the challenge of staying productive while juggling various responsibilities can be daunting. Well-being practices can provide a much-needed anchor, helping individuals navigate the tumultuous waters of a post-pandemic world.

Well-being is a holistic concept that covers physical, mental, and emotional health. Integrating practices that support these facets into one's daily routine can enhance performance and contribute to a fulfilling life. The starting point is often awareness of one's current state—identifying signs of fatigue, stress, or burnout can act as a wake-up call to start prioritizing well-being. Each practice varies in its approach, but they all share the common goal of fostering a healthier relationship between work and life.

Physical well-being can be significantly improved through regular movement and exercise. Remote workers, especially, face the drawback of potentially prolonged periods of inactivity, often seated at makeshift workspaces. Introducing short, frequent breaks for stretching or walking can dramatically enhance concentration and reduce muscle tension. Entrepreneurs and remote workers can schedule a ten-minute break every hour, embracing micro-exercises like desk yoga or a quick outdoor stroll, revitalizing the body and mind.

Nutritional intake plays a role too. Adopting mindful eating habits, like consuming balanced meals rich in proteins, vitamins, and fibers, can increase energy levels and prevent the midday slump. By planning meals in advance, they can avoid the quick reaches for unhealthy snacks during a busy day. Meal prepping saves time and cultivates a sense of routine, another pillar for balanced living.

One cannot overlook the importance of mental health as a core component of overall well-being. Mindfulness and meditation practices are gaining traction for a reason. They do not require significant time investments and can fit seamlessly into any schedule. Even five minutes of focused breathing or a guided meditation can foster a sense of calm, easing stress, and improving concentration. Mindfulness encourages a person to be present, reducing anxiety and preventing the mind from spiraling into stress over past or future events.

Emotional well-being, which often involves nurturing relationships and social connections, can be a bit trickier in remote settings. However, making it a practice to check in regularly with close friends or family, even virtually, can bolster emotional resilience. Building a community where mutual support thrives is incredibly beneficial. People can engage in activities like a virtual coffee break or participate in online seminars and workshops that focus on communication and collaboration.

Another effective strategy is maintaining a gratitude journal, a small notebook where one notes aspects of life they are grateful for each day. This practice shifts focus from stressors to positivity, enhancing emotional health. Furthermore, expressing gratitudeand appreciation towards team members or colleagues can create a supportive and encouraging work environment.

Well-Being Publishing

A key aspect of incorporating well-being practices involves managing time effectively—a challenge that's constant across all work models. Time management techniques such as the Pomodoro Technique encourage individuals to work in intervals (usually 25 minutes of focused work followed by a 5-minute break), which can prevent burnout. Tools and apps specifically designed for productivity can help maintain a balanced approach to workload management.

Equally essential is the setting of boundaries. While entire chapters could be devoted to this topic, suffice it to say, establishing clear lines between work and home life dramatically affects well-being. A dedicated workspace, regular working hours, and scheduled downtime where technology is set aside can help reinforce these boundaries. Such practices empower individuals to switch off and recharge, which ultimately boosts productivity.

Well-being doesn't stop outside the office—as social beings, our environment impacts us. Hence, optimizing the workspace to promote well-being can lead to tangible improvements in productivity. A clean, organized space paired with personal touches, like plants or photos, can lift spirits. Incorporating ergonomic desks and chairs reduces physical strain and creates a conducive atmosphere for productivity.

For managers and HR professionals, encouraging and facilitating these practices within their teams is crucial. Whether it's through providing access to wellness programs, organizing regular team-building activities, or offering mental health days, leadership plays a pivotal role. On a larger scale, companies can incorporate work-life balance guides into their onboarding processes, highlighting the organization's commitment to employee well-being.

Ultimately, well-being practices are not one-size-fits-all. Each individual may have differing needs and responses based on personal circumstances and professional demands. The key is to experiment and cultivate a toolkit of practices that resonate personally. The pursuit of balance is ongoing, and regular adjustments ensure that the craft of enhancing productivity and well-being is continually honed.

Incorporating well-being into daily habits may not immediately eradicate all stressors of modern work-life, but it provides a sturdy foundation to build resilience and achieve sustained productivity. By treating well-being as a continuous process rather than a quick fix, individuals can adapt and thrive in an ever-changing world.

Chapter 7:
Technology and Balance

In our rapidly evolving digital landscape, finding equilibrium between technology use and personal well-being has become an intricate dance. As remote work continues to redefine boundaries, gadgets and apps offer unprecedented ways to stay connected and boost productivity. Yet, inadvertently, they can also blur the line between work and rest, leading to digital fatigue. It's essential to harness technology wisely, ensuring it enhances rather than disrupts our work-life harmony. By setting intentional digital boundaries and embracing mindful tech habits, individuals can transform potential digital chaos into an ally for achieving balance. This chapter delves into strategies for leveraging technology effectively without falling prey to burnout, providing a roadmap for integrating tech into a balanced life without compromising on personal well-being.

Leveraging Technology for Balance

In the quest for work-life balance, technology stands as both ally and adversary. It offers a suite of tools that can transform the chaotic into the manageable, yet it can also encroach on personal boundaries if not handled with care. Striking the right balance involves utilizing technology in ways that foster efficiency and provide the freedom needed to focus on life's other demands. This section explores how to harness technology to improve balance without falling into the trap of digital overload.

Remote work, once a luxury or an exception, is now a mainstay of contemporary employment. The time and commute it saves are undeniable gains, but it also means that work can follow us everywhere, encroaching on personal time. It's vital to establish clear lines of demarcation between work hours and personal time. Using scheduling apps effectively and setting 'Do Not Disturb' modes on devices can create a barrier that ensures life outside work retains its sanctity.

Task management software has evolved into a lifeline for those juggling myriad responsibilities. Applications like Trello and Monday.com allow an individual to visualize tasks, delegate effectively, and keep track of daily, weekly, or even monthly goals. These tools help focus one's energy on what truly matters, allowing the less critical tasks to be handled asynchronously or at a time that's less intrusive to personal life.

Moreover, the advent of digital communication platforms such as Slack and Microsoft Teams provide avenues for collaboration without the need for tedious email chains or cumbersome meetings. Used judiciously, these platforms can streamline communication, allowing quick problem resolution and idea exchange without adding to stress. The caveat, however, is setting strong communication protocols to avoid the expectation of 24/7 availability.

Automation represents another technology facet that can reclaim precious time. Simple tasks, whether sending routine emails or posting on social media, can be automated to free up mental bandwidth for more significant problems or creative pursuits. Mastering the use of tools like Zapier or IFTTT can make a substantial difference in everyday workflow efficiency.

However, technology should also facilitate downtime rather than constantly be a source of engagement. Several apps promote mindfulness and relaxation, helping to mitigate stress and enhance general well-being. Applications like Headspace and Calm provide accessible guided meditations and mindfulness exercises, helping users unplug and center themselves effectively after a hectic day of work.

Wearable technology also plays a role in maintaining a balance between professional and personal life. Fitness trackers and smartwatches keep tabs on physical activity, reminding users to move and take breaks from sedentary work. With sedentary lifestyles becoming a norm in technology-driven work environments, integrating these devices can help maintain both physical health and mental clarity.

The importance of a well-designed workspace can't be overstated, and technology can complement this. Ergonomic furniture coupled with items like standing desks and adjustable monitors can reduce physical strain, improving comfort and productivity. However, it boils down to personal preferences and needs, emphasizing comfortable yet conducive settings for prolonged usage of technological tools.

In facilitating better balance, adopting cloud storage and project management tools provides an additional layer of flexibility. With clouds, like Google Drive and Dropbox, accessing work files or applications from any device is seamless, eliminating the need to carry everything everywhere physically. This accessibility can reduce anxiety about being away from a primary workspace.

Notwithstanding the conveniences digital workflows may bring, technology needs to be actively managed. Implementing deliberate disconnects—such as scheduled logging off from work accounts—ensures that leisure time is truly 'off the clock'. Creating tech-free zones in home environments can also safeguard family and personal time, reducing the temptation to drift back into work during relaxation hours.

Lastly, continuous upskilling in digital literacies allows individuals to better utilize the technologies available. Understanding the potential of each tool and the efficiencies it can introduce into one's life can greatly impact how balance is maintained. Many online platforms offer educational content aimed at improving digital skills, which can enhance the effectiveness of technology use in promoting balance.

The journey to balance, much like using technology, requires a conscientious approach realizing that what works for one may not fit another. Therefore, customizing tech solutions to fit individual lifestyles is critical. In doing so, individuals can leverage technology not as a burden, but as a springboard to a healthier, more balanced existence.

Avoiding Technology Burnout

In our hyper-connected world, technology has become a double-edged sword. On one side, it offers unprecedented convenience and efficiency; on the other, it threatens to overwhelm and exhaust us. The very tools designed to enhance productivity often end up consuming our mental and emotional resources. For remote workers, entrepreneurs, and anyone trying to strike a balance between professional responsibilities and personal life, the challenge lies in how to harness technology without falling prey to its demands.

A crucial step in avoiding technology burnout is to actively set limits on how we interact with technology. Constant notifications, endless email threads, and the pressure to be always "on" can blur the lines between work and leisure. Therefore, establishing digital boundaries becomes essential. Consider setting specific times during the day to check emails and social media rather than responding to each ping. Creating these boundaries not only helps manage your time effectively but also allows your mind the respite it desperately needs.

Think of time away from screens as time for mental decluttering. Scheduling "unplugged" sessions, where technology is not within arm's reach, can be incredibly refreshing. These breaks allow you to reconnect with activities often neglected, like a face-to-face conversation over coffee, a walk in the park, or reading a book. Not only does this practice rejuvenate your mental faculties, but it also strengthens your connection with the world outside the digital realm.

Mindfulness practices offer powerful antidotes to technology burnout as well. Integrate short mindfulness exercises into your daily routine. Even a few minutes of meditation or deep-breathing exercises can center your thoughts and refocus your energy. These practices help you cultivate a heightened awareness of your technology consumption, enabling you to make more conscious choices.

The modern work environment, especially post-pandemic, often demands multi-device juggling. To counteract the potential stress from this requirement, streamline your digital workspace. Employ productivity tools designed to enhance focus and reduce digital noise. Applications that block non-essential websites during work hours or tools that allow you to batch process tasks can drastically reduce digital clutter.

Human interaction is another area often sacrificed at the altar of technology. Yet, it plays a crucial role in maintaining balance and preventing burnout. In a work-from-home scenario, it's easy to fall into the trap of isolation. Actively seek out moments of genuine connection, whether through virtual coffee breaks with colleagues or networking opportunities within your community. By nurturing social interactions, you create support systems that foster emotional resilience.

Additionally, let technology itself be part of the solution. Digital wellness apps can track and analyze your tech usage patterns, offering insights and encouraging healthier habits. These tools often come equipped with features that alert you to excessive usage and suggest intervals to take breaks, practicing what they preach through their own functioning.

Another effective way to navigate technology burnout is by prioritizing purpose-driven technology usage. Engage with technology consciously—ask yourself what adds value to your life and what merely consumes attention without offering much in return. This aspect ties in with developing digital literacy that doesn't just focus on the skills to use technology but also the wisdom to use it wisely.

For working parents, the challenge can be particularly intense. Technology, while essential for managing both professional and personal schedules, can also become a source of distraction from family life. Setting an example for children by demonstrating healthy tech habits highlights the importance of being present without the constant intrusion of screens. Involve children in activities that don't require gadgets, fostering a family culture that appreciates offline joys.

Entrepreneurs too, often find themselves tethered to their gadgets as they build and grow their enterprises. It's easy to equate constant connectivity with dedication and progress. However, understanding that creative insights often arise away from screens can liberate entrepreneurs from tech over-dependence. Allow yourself time away from technology to brainstorm and reflect—it may lead to breakthroughs that endless hours online might not provide.

Managers and HR professionals also play a vital role in managing technology burnout within organizational cultures. Encouraging employees to take time off, promoting a healthy balance between online and offline tasks, and creating a workplace environment that values human interaction over digital interaction are important steps toward collective well-being.

Ultimately, avoiding technology burnout is about regaining control—being proactive rather than reactive. It involves a conscious decision to steer technology use to serve you, rather than allowing it to dictate your routines and emotions. By implementing mindful strategies and embracing the potential for change, we can redefine our relationship with technology, ensuring it's an enabler of our goals and well-being rather than an impediment.

Chapter 8:
Supporting Working Parents

Balancing the responsibilities of work and parenting can feel like a high-wire act, fraught with challenges, yet simultaneously filled with opportunities for growth and connection. Working parents, often the keystone of family structures, face unique pressures as they navigate demanding professional landscapes alongside the ever-evolving needs of their children. Addressing these challenges requires comprehensive support systems, both in the workplace and at home. Employers can create more accommodating environments by integrating flexible work schedules, offering parental leave policies, and fostering a culture where open dialogue about needs and expectations is encouraged. At the same time, a strong network of family, friends, and community resources can provide much-needed emotional and logistical support. The synthesis of these strategies not only helps parents to thrive professionally but also enriches their personal lives, enabling them to be present and engaged with their families. Ultimately, by prioritizing the well-being of working parents, organizations cultivate a dedicated, resilient workforce that is capable of achieving remarkable feats, both at work and in their personal spheres.

Challenges Faced by Working Parents

Being a working parent today is like walking a tightrope; one wrong move can send everything you've juggled crashing down. The integration of professional responsibilities with the unending demands of parenthood can often feel akin to managing dual, full-time jobs. Unlike past generations, today's working parents face unique challenges exacerbated by technological advancements, societal expectations, and the unpredictable nature of modern work environments. While many companies are moving towards more flexible working conditions post-pandemic, the underlying challenges for working parents have merely shifted.

A predominant challenge is the blurred boundary between home and work. With the rise of remote work, the absence of a physical divide between job and personal life means that work tasks and parenting tasks often overlap. Imagine responding to urgent emails while trying to assist your child with homework, or worse, attending a crucial meeting only to be interrupted by a playful toddler. This overlapping of domains raises not just logistical issues but a mental strain of trying to be present in two demanding roles simultaneously. The absence of commutes, which once acted as a buffer zone to transition between these two worlds, means many parents feel "always on," with little time for personal rest.

Time management is another significant hurdle. The traditional nine-to-five model rarely aligns with school hours or daycare operations, creating a constant scramble for childcare solutions or after-school activities. Flexibility in work hours is welcomed but can complicate collaboration with colleagues who might have different schedules. Single parents, in particular, feel the pressure doubly, often lacking a co-parent to share responsibilities, making them perpetually pressed for time and attention. Despite the presence of technology offering tools for scheduling and productivity, many find themselves ensnared by the paradox of increased connectivity leading to greater demands.

Moreover, the societal pressure to "do it all" weighs heavily. Social media has only heightened the ideals of perfect parenting and professional success, creating an invisible bar that many feel compelled to reach. This results in feelings of inadequacy when parents perceive themselves as falling short on either front. Furthermore, gender roles still subtly manifest in workplace attitudes, with mothers often expected to prioritize home responsibilities, whereas fathers can face biases when they seek flexibility for family commitments. Such societal constructs compound the stress and lead to guilt and sometimes workplace discrimination.

Access to adequate support systems—or the lack thereof—can make or break the experience for working parents. Those with access to extensive family networks or affordable childcare might face different stressors than those without such support. Additionally, the quality of childcare services varies greatly, and financially, it can be equivalent to a second mortgage for many families. The relentless search for reliable and safe childcare is another layer of stress that working parents often contend with. Not to mention, in many places, the policies surrounding parental leave remain archaic, providing neither enough time nor resources to facilitate a smooth career transition post-childbirth.

Engaging with work during personal time speaks to an increasing concern over technology's role in work-life balance. Parents often find themselves logging back into work after putting the kids to bed, pushing their workdays late into the night, leading to burnout. They juggle between ensuring their visibility at work and being present for their children, leading to a dilution in the quality of engagement on both ends. The pressure to constantly demonstrate productivity can further spur feelings of stress and inadequacy.

Then there are the emotional and psychological aspects. The sheer exhaustion from managing numerous to-do lists daily can lead to stress-induced health issues. Many parents battle with feelings of guilt over perceived neglect of family or career duties. The cycle of guilt and pressure can erode mental health, leading to anxiety or depression. The expectation to sustain efficiency at work while nurturing a thriving home environment is a colossal task, leading many to compromise either on rest or hobbies. Parents who attempt to equally excel seem to pay with their well-being.

Finally, school-related challenges take up a substantial portion of a working parent's bandwidth. Unscheduled early dismissals, sporting events, and school meetings often clash with work commitments. Balancing presence at such important events without losing ground in their careers demands constant strategic juggling. The pandemic has further highlighted this with sudden school closures and the switch to virtual classrooms, forcing parents into roles of impromptu educators or supervisors, a task many feel unequipped to handle.

In sum, working parents face a complex web of challenges that test their resilience and adaptability daily. It isn't merely about balancing two roles but about constantly adjusting their expectations and strategies in response to a society that is evolving but still rooted in traditional constructs. Addressing these challenges requires a nuanced approach—understanding from employers, flexible work cultures, equitable gender role attitudes, supportive government policies on parental leave, and stronger community networks. In the chapters to follow, we'll explore solutions and systems that can equip working parents with the tools they need to thrive, rather than just survive, in their dual roles.

Support Systems and Solutions for Parents

As the realm of work-life balance continues to evolve, one group that faces unique challenges is working parents. Balancing the responsibilities of a career and raising children can be daunting, especially in a world that demands continuous adaptation to new work environments and schedules. The hustle and bustle of modern life can make it seem impossible to meet all obligations without compromising on either side. However, with the right support systems and tailored solutions, the journey can be made significantly more manageable and fulfilling.

One crucial element in crafting effective support systems for working parents is leveraging community resources. Local community centers, parenting groups, and even neighborhood organizations often provide invaluable support ranging from parenting workshops to child-friendly events that enable parents to connect and share experiences. These networks create a sense of belonging and offer practical advice that can be transformational in a parent's journey. Moreover, understanding that you're not alone in facing these challenges can be both comforting and empowering.

Workplace solutions also play a pivotal role. Organizations that recognize the pressures faced by working parents often implement programs that provide leeway, such as flexible working hours and remote work options. Offering part-time positions or job-sharing arrangements can also create a more adaptable work environment for parents. Additionally, on-site childcare facilities or partnerships with local daycare centers can greatly alleviate the stress of managing daily routines. By supporting such initiatives, companies not only assist their employees but also promote a culture of inclusivity and understanding.

Technology offers another avenue for support that parents can tap into. Apps designed to streamline family schedules, meal planning, and even educational activities for children, can shave minutes off a parent's day-to-day tasks and make the workload seem less burdensome. Scheduling automation, digital to-do lists, and shared family calendars can transform chaos into a manageable routine, allowing parents to concentrate on spending quality time with their families rather than juggling endless tasks.

Furthermore, the involvement of partners in parenting duties is essential to achieving balance and reducing stress. Open communication and shared responsibilities — ranging from managing school commitments to house chores — can help relieve the pressure often felt by one partner bearing the majority of the obligations. Whether it's alternating school drop-offs or taking turns to prepare meals, the support of a partner can significantly impact a parent's ability to enjoy their dual roles.

Extended family and friends can be another pillar of support. Grandparents, uncles, aunts, and close family friends can sometimes provide childcare, mentorship, or simply a sympathetic ear. Having a support network that parents can rely on, whether occasionally or regularly, enriches family life and provides parents with the opportunity to manage their careers without neglecting household duties or personal well-being.

Self-care is yet another critical component that should not be overlooked. While managing professional responsibilities and parenting can consume most of a parent's time, prioritizing personal well-being ensures sustainability over the long haul. Whether it's scheduling regular exercise, ensuring enough sleep, or simply taking alone time to unwind and regroup, self-care strategies empower parents to be present and engaged with their families while maintaining productivity at work.

Finally, seeking professional guidance can be a valuable step for parents feeling overwhelmed or struggling to maintain equilibrium. Life coaches, family therapists, and career counselors can provide targeted strategies to help redesign a balanced lifestyle. Sometimes an external perspective can offer fresh insights and actionable approaches that might not be evident amidst the daily grind.

In summary, the keys to effectively supporting working parents lie in crafting a multi-faceted approach that combines community involvement, organizational support, technological aids, and personal strategies. By fostering a supportive network and accessing available resources, working parents can successfully navigate the intricacies of combining work and family life. The end goal is to create a nurturing environment that encourages both personal and professional growth, without sacrificing one for the other.

Chapter 9: Strategies for Entrepreneurs

For entrepreneurs navigating the tumultuous waters of modern business, finding a rhythm between passion and practicality is key. While the allure of self-driven ventures provides unparalleled freedom, it also demands a resilience that's bolstered by effective strategies for work-life balance. Successful entrepreneurs often start by setting clear priorities, ensuring personal values align with business goals to avoid the perils of burnout. They embrace delegation, understanding it's not just about lessening their workload but also empowering their teams to grow. Time management becomes an art, where leveraging tools to automate and optimize routines can transform daily chaos into structured efficiency. Networking, too, isn't merely about expanding business but also about nurturing a support system that shares insights and experiences. These strategies ultimately allow entrepreneurs to maintain their passion, ensuring that their ventures are sustainable and fulfilling in the long run.

Balance Tips for Entrepreneurs

Entrepreneurship often feels like a 24/7 job. Between balancing growth strategies and handling unforeseen challenges, entrepreneurs may find their work consuming every waking moment. It's essential, though, to maintain a healthy balance between your professional and personal life. Finding harmony can help you stay inspired and avoid the all-too-common burnout that plagues many in this demanding field.

Harmony at Hand

First and foremost, recognizing the importance of dividing your time effectively is crucial. Create a schedule that respects both your business needs and personal priorities. Use tools like digital calendars to set clear work hours. Dynamic scheduling—allocating slots for deep work, meetings, and personal tasks—can make a world of difference. The key is to stick to it religiously. By designating specific times for work and leisure, you ensure neither is neglected.

A novel strategy is compartmentalizing tasks. Rather than facing a fragmented array of responsibilities at once, organize tasks by categories and tackle them in succession. For instance, dedicate mornings to strategic planning and afternoons to operational tasks. This minimizes the mental burden of switching between vastly different thought processes, allowing for a more streamlined and effective day.

Delegation often proves challenging, but it's a fundamental component in achieving balance. Entrusting tasks to capable team members not only frees up your time but also empowers your staff. Start by identifying tasks that can be delegated and find reliable personnel to handle them. Effective delegation extends your reach without stretching your resources thin and encourages a collaborative team culture.

Entrepreneurs must also learn to tap into the power of technology. Automation can streamline repetitive tasks and free up valuable time. Identify areas in your business that can benefit from automated solutions such as social media scheduling tools or customer service bots. Implementing these technologies can help you focus on tasks that truly require your personal attention.

However, technology can be a double-edged sword. While it aids productivity, it can also lead to burnout if not managed properly. Set boundaries on device usage, especially during personal time. Consider implementing technology-free zones or times in your day to disconnect and recharge. This simple act can significantly improve mental well-being and overall productivity.

Moreover, nurturing creativity is vital for sustaining passion in entrepreneurship. Make time for activities that inspire you or let your mind wander. Whether it's a hobby, reading, or even taking walks—these activities rejuvenate the mind and enhance problem-solving abilities. A fresh perspective often emerges when you're not actively seeking it, which can be invaluable for your business.

Mental health, though sometimes overlooked, needs attention too. Establish a routine that incorporates mental wellness practices like mindfulness or meditation. These practices can significantly reduce stress and improve focus. Regular breaks to stretch or take a walk can also prevent fatigue and maintain productivity throughout the day.

It's important to mention the value of a support network. Connect with other entrepreneurs through networks or mastermind groups. Sharing challenges and successes with peers who understand your journey can provide fresh insights and emotional support. Not only do these relationships foster new business opportunities, but they also create a sense of community, reducing the isolation that sometimes accompanies entrepreneurship.

Finally, never underestimate the power of saying no. Opportunities often come knocking, but not all of them align with your long-term goals. Learning to discern which ventures to pursue and which to decline is essential. Protect your time and resources by focusing on activities that drive growth and align with your vision. Carefully evaluate each opportunity, weighing its potential benefits against its demands on your time and energy.

In conclusion, striking a balance is not about dividing your time equally but about creating a life where your business and personal pursuits thrive alongside each other. Incorporating these strategies can lead to a more fulfilling entrepreneurial journey, characterized by sustained enthusiasm and a reduced risk of burnout. Remember, achieving balance is an ongoing process, requiring periodic reassessment and adjustments. Your business will benefit from a healthier, happier you, and that's a strategy that pays dividends in the long run.

Maintaining Passion Without Burnout

As entrepreneurs, the drive to innovate and succeed is often matched by an equally strong risk of burnout. Passion fuels the journey, but without careful management, it can lead to exhaustion and disengagement. For those venturing in this relentless domain, maintaining enthusiasm without overstepping into burnout territory requires deliberate strategies and conscious choices.

Firstly, it's crucial to understand that passion is a renewable resource, not an exhaustible one. Just like keeping a fire alive, your passion needs both fuel and oxygen. The right fuel consists of goals aligned with your core values and a clear vision of what you aim to achieve. Oxygen, on the other hand, comes from stepping back, taking breaks, and allowing space for reflection. This dual approach keeps the flame burning brightly without being snuffed out by continuous stress.

Another fundamental aspect is embracing the importance of delegation. Entrepreneurs often wear multiple hats, which can be exciting but also overwhelming. By learning to delegate effectively, you can focus on the tasks that truly ignite your passion, while entrusting other responsibilities to capable team members. This not only prevents burnout but also empowers your team, fostering a culture of trust and collaboration.

A supportive network is invaluable in this process. Surrounding yourself with like-minded individuals who understand your journey can provide both inspiration and practical advice. Whether it's through mentorship, professional groups, or peer discussions, these connections offer both an outlet for sharing challenges and a source of encouragement. It's an opportunity to learn from others' experiences and to reaffirm that you're not alone on this winding path.

Moreover, maintaining a routine that prioritizes well-being is essential. This doesn't simply mean exercising or eating right, although those are critical. It involves a holistic approach that includes mental and emotional health. Practices such as mindfulness or meditation can offer ways to ground yourself, reducing stress and increasing clarity. Incorporating these into daily routines transforms them from an afterthought to a non-negotiable element of success.

The art of saying "no" can't be overstated. Entrepreneurs often encounter a barrage of opportunities and requests. It may feel counterintuitive, but learning to decline certain ventures that don't align with your passion or current focus is crucial. This selective approach ensures that your attention and energy are directed towards projects that genuinely matter to you and your business.

Understanding personal limits is another key factor in this balance. Recognizing when to push forward and when to step back is an art. For some, it means setting defined work hours or using reminders to log off, while for others it might involve taking a mental health day or planning regular vacations. The essential part is finding and respecting your limits to prevent pushing into burnout territory.

To sustain passion, entrepreneurs should also commit to lifelong learning. Gaining new skills or perspectives can recharge your enthusiasm and keep your business on the cutting edge. Whether it's through formal education, online courses, or self-guided learning, constantly evolving ensures that you stay invigorated and engaged.

Lastly, celebrate small wins and progress. In the pursuit of big goals, it's easy to overlook the smaller, incremental successes that make up the journey. Recognizing and celebrating these achievements provides motivation and a sense of satisfaction that keeps passion alive. This approach fosters a positive mindset and reinforces the value of persistence.

In summation, maintaining passion without succumbing to burnout is a delicate balance that requires intentional actions and a mindful approach. By fueling passion with aligned goals, delegating wisely, and integrating self-care into daily habits, entrepreneurs can navigate this challenging road with resilience and sustained enthusiasm. It's this blend of strategic management and personal well-being that not only protects your passion but allows it to flourish in the long term.

Chapter 10: Leadership and Management Approaches

Leadership in today's evolving work landscape requires a fine balance between guiding teams towards achieving organizational goals and nurturing an environment where employees feel supported and valued. Managers and leaders are increasingly called to adopt approaches that not only prioritize productivity but also consider the well-being and work-life balance of their teams. Successful leaders leverage empathy and open communication, encouraging a culture of trust and flexibility. This enables employees to thrive and be more resilient in the face of challenges. Policies that support mental health and offer flexibility—like remote work options and mental health days—serve as crucial tools for modern-day leadership. Progressive management approaches recognize that when employees are supported holistically, they're not just more productive; they're more engaged and loyal. Crafting a workplace environment where balance is celebrated rather than sacrificed requires intentional leadership focused on long-term well-being, ensuring that no one has to choose between personal life and professional achievements.

Leadership Strategies for Team Balance

In the evolving landscape of remote and hybrid work environments, achieving team balance has quickly become a focal point for leaders. In our quest to understand how leaders can effectively manage diversity in work styles, it is crucial to first recognize the unique challenges that teams face in this new era. Leaders must juggle the demands of productivity while fostering a supportive and inclusive atmosphere where every team member feels valued and engaged. The integration of work-life balance principles into team management offers a pathway to not only enhance employee satisfaction but also bolster team performance.

The cornerstone of achieving team balance lies in the leader's ability to clearly define and communicate the team's goals while being mindful of individual responsibilities and circumstances. Leaders should embark on this journey by establishing clear yet flexible objectives that allow team members to align personal and professional ambitions seamlessly. This mix of structure and flexibility can be initiated through regular team meetings where goals are discussed openly, and everyone's input is considered. By fostering such an environment, leaders mitigate the tensions that often arise when business priorities clash with personal commitments.

Another key strategy is cultivating a culture of openness and trust within the team. Leaders who encourage authenticity help create an environment where team members feel comfortable sharing personal challenges that might affect their work. By actively listening and addressing these concerns, leaders contribute to the development of robust support systems that enhance team dynamics. Further, building trust involves demonstrating reliability and openness to feedback, which can significantly reduce stress and promote a healthy work-life balance for everyone involved.

Empowerment is yet another significant component. When leaders delegate responsibilities effectively, they not only distribute the workload evenly but also empower team members to take ownership of their roles. This empowerment can be achieved by identifying individual strengths and aligning them with team tasks, giving employees the chance to shine in their areas of expertise. Confidence grows when employees are trusted with their responsibilities, leading to higher job satisfaction and reduced burnout.

Effective communication plays a pivotal role in maintaining team balance. Timely and clear communication helps prevent misunderstandings and ensures that everyone is on the same page regarding expectations and deadlines. Leaders can create various channels for communication, such as weekly check-ins, group chats, or collaborative platforms like Slack or Microsoft Teams. Utilizing these tools effectively ensures that team members can share updates or concerns without unnecessary delays.

Leaders should also focus on developing emotional intelligence. Understanding and managing one's emotions, as well as the emotions of others, can drastically improve interpersonal interactions within the team. A leader who demonstrates empathy can recognize the emotional states of team members and adjust strategies accordingly. For instance, acknowledging the extra pressures an employee might be facing can go a long way in showing support and fostering trust in the team dynamic.

Encouraging continuous professional development and personal growth is also instrumental in maintaining team balance. Leaders should create opportunities for team members to engage in training, workshops, or mentorship programs that align with their career aspirations. Such initiatives not only enhance skills but also communicate to team members that their growth and well-being are valued. This can translate into higher motivation levels, with team members feeling more committed and enthusiastic about their roles.

Another strategy to consider is recognizing and celebrating successes, both big and small. Whether it's meeting a project deadline or achieving a significant milestone, acknowledging these efforts can boost morale and foster a sense of accomplishment. Celebrations could range from a simple shout-out during a meeting to organizing virtual or physical get-togethers to mark milestone achievements. Recognition of hard work reinforces positive behavior and motivates others to strive for excellence.

Leaders can also adopt a results-oriented approach where the emphasis is on output rather than the hours clocked. By focusing on results, leaders allow team members to manage their time efficiently, resulting in less stress and more balanced workdays. Flexible working hours, for instance, can be a great way to honor employees' personal time while still expecting them to meet deadlines consistently. This shows an understanding of diverse work rhythms and personal circumstances.

Finally, leaders must remember the importance of modeling work-life balance themselves. By setting an example in prioritizing self-care and personal time, leaders convey the message that it is acceptable and necessary to maintain balance. Whether it's not sending emails after work hours or taking regular leave for personal matters, such actions speak volumes and encourage the team to also pursue balance.

In conclusion, leadership strategies for achieving team balance are not just beneficial for employees, they are integral to fostering a thriving work environment where innovation and productivity can flourish. By adopting these strategies, leaders can navigate the complexities of modern work environments with agility, ensuring that work-life balance is achieved not at the expense of performance, but to enhance and sustain it.

Implementing Employee Supportive Policies

In the evolving landscape of work and life integration, implementing employee supportive policies isn't just a management strategy; it's a necessity. Organizations that prioritize these policies create an environment where employees feel valued and supported, leading to enhanced productivity and well-being. A company's leadership plays a critical role in this implementation. By understanding the needs of their workforce, leaders can design policies that are not only practical but beneficial in promoting a healthy work-life balance.

Employee supportive policies should be grounded in flexibility. In today's fast-paced world, the one-size-fits-all approach is outdated. Workers thrive in environments that accommodate their individual needs, whether they're new parents, remote workers, or someone recovering from burnout. Allowing flexible work hours or the option to telecommute can greatly reduce stress, making employees feel in control of their work and personal lives. When employees have the autonomy to adjust their schedules, they are more likely to be engaged and committed to their jobs.

Another key aspect of supportive policies is the promotion of mental health. As stress levels rise, companies must be proactive in providing resources that support mental well-being. Employers might consider offering counseling services, stress management workshops, or mindfulness programs. Creating a culture that talks openly about mental health encourages employees to seek help when needed without fear of stigma.

Financial wellness should also be addressed within employee supportive policies. Financial stress can be a significant burden on employees, impacting their productivity and focus. Implementing programs such as financial literacy workshops, retirement planning, and student loan assistance can empower employees to take charge of their financial health. These initiatives reflect an organization's commitment to its workforce's holistic well-being.

Providing opportunities for professional development can be incredibly motivating and rewarding for employees. Whether through mentorship programs, leadership training, or tuition assistance, investing in employees' growth shows that the company values not only their current contributions but also their future potential.

Promoting work-life balance is also about creating a culture where taking time off is encouraged. Policies that provide adequate paid time off (PTO), parental leave, or even sabbaticals can prevent employee burnout. It's crucial to create an environment where taking leave is seen as a right, not a taboo. When leaders model this behavior by taking time off themselves, it sends a powerful message that rest and rejuvenation are essential components of a sustainable work-life balance.

Communication is the backbone of implementing any employee supportive policy. Leaders must ensure that policies are clearly communicated and easy to understand. Open channels should exist for employees to voice their needs or concerns about existing policies. Feedback loops are invaluable for making continuous improvements to policies, ensuring they remain relevant and effective in meeting the evolving needs of the workforce.

A culturally diverse workplace requires culturally sensitive employee support policies. Policies should be inclusive and free from bias, considering the different cultural backgrounds of employees. It is essential that these policies are not only written inclusively but also practiced inclusively so every employee feels respected and valued in the workspace.

For working parents, policies that offer onsite childcare, remote work options, or flexible schedules can make balancing work and family responsibilities more manageable. By accommodating the unique needs of parents, organizations can retain valuable talent and reduce turnover rates. Implementing family-friendly policies is not just beneficial for employees but can lead to enhanced loyalty and commitment to the organization.

Additionally, as remote work becomes increasingly common, policies must adapt to this reality. Virtual team-building activities, regular check-ins, and digital collaboration tools can help maintain a sense of community and ensure remote employees feel just as connected and valued as their in-office counterparts. Ensuring equity between remote and office workers is vital in maintaining workforce morale.

The cornerstone of any policy implementation should be trust and empowerment. Empowering employees to make decisions related to their workflow and personal needs fosters an environment of trust. When employees feel trusted, they are more likely to take ownership of their roles and responsibilities, ultimately benefiting the organization as a whole.

Finally, it's important for companies to periodically review and update their employee supportive policies. The workplace is ever-changing, and policies need to be agile enough to keep pace with these changes. Continuous assessment and adaptation ensure that the policies serve the intended purpose of supporting employees in achieving a harmonious work-life balance.

By creating a supportive environment through thoughtful policies, organizations not only enhance employee satisfaction and productivity but also cultivate a resilient and loyal workforce ready to thrive in a dynamic work environment. Leadership's role is instrumental in crafting and promoting these policies, aligning with the overarching goal to create a sustainable work-life balance for all.

Chapter 11:
HR's Role in Work-Life Harmony

In today's evolving workplace, HR professionals find themselves at the forefront of fostering work-life harmony, a crucial element in curbing burnout and enhancing employee satisfaction. They don't just create policies; they cultivate environments where flexibility and balance are more than buzzwords—they're lived experiences. By strategically developing HR policies that prioritize employee wellness and encourage an open dialogue about personal needs, HR can initiate profound culture shifts within organizations. This involves nurturing an atmosphere of trust and mutual respect, where employees feel empowered to voice their needs and are met with support rather than resistance. Encouraging such a culture isn't just beneficial—it's vital for organizations eager to thrive in the post-pandemic landscape, adapting to hybrid work setups and diverse employee expectations. In essence, HR acts as the catalyst for evolution, ensuring that the quest for balance becomes an organizational priority rather than a personal battle.

Developing HR Policies for Balance

It's crucial for organizations to recognize the evolving landscape of work and step up with programs that genuinely promote work-life harmony. Human Resources (HR) departments serve as the strategic architects in designing policies that not only support employees but also align with the broader organizational goals. Let's delve into how

HR can craft policies that meet the needs of a modern, diverse workforce.

One of the first steps HR can take is conducting comprehensive needs assessments. By actively engaging with employees through surveys, focus groups, or suggestion boxes, companies can gain insight into what truly matters to their workforce. Whether it's flexible working hours, mental health resources, or parental leave policies, these insights guide the design of impactful HR programs. Clearly, a one-size-fits-all approach doesn't cut it anymore. Companies need to be attuned to various needs and preferences.

An ideal HR policy acknowledges that flexibility is central to work-life balance. Remote and hybrid working options have become invaluable, yet they introduce unique challenges that HR must navigate. Policies must clearly outline expectations, setting parameters to help manage remote work without the risk of burnout. Structured flexibility not only boosts employee morale but also enhances overall productivity. Encouraging managers to trust their teams and focus on outcomes rather than the number of hours worked is also instrumental.

Furthermore, implementing policies that support mental health is no longer optional—it's a necessity. HR must champion initiatives that bring mental well-being into the spotlight, eroding the stigma often associated with mental health discussions. Providing access to virtual therapy sessions, promoting mental health days, or encouraging involvement in stress-reduction programs can profoundly impact employees' overall well-being. HR's role extends beyond policy creation; it also involves building a support network that reassures employees that their mental health is a priority.

Training managers to embody and enforce these policies is another critical aspect. Managers act as the frontline ambassadors of HR policies; thus, they should be equipped to foster a culture of balance within their teams. Leadership workshops and ongoing training can ensure managers are adept at identifying signs of burnout, offering support, and reducing the stigma around seeking help. When managers model a balanced approach, it resonates throughout the team.

A robust HR policy must also encompass comprehensive leave policies. Generous parental leave, compassionate leave, and sabbaticals demonstrate a company's commitment to its employees' personal needs and life events. These offerings not only attract top talent but also elevate employee satisfaction, which reduces turnover. When employees feel valued and respected for their commitments both within and outside work, they're more likely to engage meaningfully with their roles.

Equipping the workforce with skills to manage their work-life balance is just as important. HR departments can introduce educational workshops and resources that teach time management, effective communication, and boundary-setting skills. Exploring partnerships with wellness experts to conduct sessions on mindfulness or stress management could also benefit employees. When staff members are empowered with tools to take control of their balance, they function optimally.

HR also plays a crucial role in promoting a culture of inclusion and diversity. Policies should ensure that all employees, regardless of their circumstances, feel supported. This includes creating spaces for open dialogue on challenges diverse employees face and ensuring that policies are inclusive of various family structures, lifestyle choices, and personal needs. Inclusivity empowers all employees to pursue balance authentically, without fear of judgment or exclusion.

Periodic reviews and iterations of HR policies are essential. With work dynamics continually shifting, a stagnant policy can lead to dissatisfaction and disengagement. Regular feedback loops and performance metrics can help assess if policies meet their intended objectives or need recalibrating. Additionally, benchmarking against industry standards can provide insight into innovative practices that can be adopted for further improvement.

Ultimately, the success of these policies relies heavily on transparent communication. Organizations must ensure that employees are well-informed about the available resources and options. Clear, consistent messaging across all channels guarantees that employees understand how to access and benefit from these policies. Facilitating forums or Q&A sessions where employees can voice concerns or seek clarifications can further enhance this transparency.

To conclude, developing HR policies for balance is a delicate endeavor that requires a data-driven, empathetic approach. With the proper foundation, HR can foster an environment that not only champions productivity and organizational success but also prioritizes the well-being of its greatest asset—its people. In the end, creating a harmonious work-life balance culture lays the groundwork for a thriving, resilient workforce prepared to face the challenges of the ever-changing work landscape.

Encouraging Organizational Culture Change

Organizational culture plays a pivotal role in shaping how employees experience work-life balance. It's like the invisible hand that guides behavior and sets the tone for what's acceptable within a workplace. For HR professionals looking to foster a culture that champions work-life harmony, the task begins with a clear understanding of what culture actually entails. It's the shared values, beliefs, and assumptions that bind members of an organization together—a collective ethos that influences everything from major decisions to everyday interactions.

To truly encourage organizational culture change, HR must start by assessing the current culture. This involves gathering insights about what employees believe the organization stands for and identifying any gaps between the company's stated values and the lived experiences of its people. Surveys, focus groups, and one-on-one conversations can offer HR an authentic view of the current climate and help pinpoint areas where work-life balance initiatives align with or diverge from existing cultural norms.

Once there's a clear picture of the existing culture, the next step is envisioning what a balanced culture ought to look like. This vision should align with the organization's goals and values while also promoting employee well-being. It requires a strategic shift that acknowledges the diverse needs of the workforce—whether they include flexible hours for working parents or opportunities for remote work to reduce commute stress. The aim is to craft an environment where balance isn't just encouraged—it's ingrained in the fabric of daily operations.

HR professionals need to lead by example. Leadership endorsement is crucial for cultural initiatives to take root. When leaders model behaviors that support work-life balance, it sends a powerful message that such practices are valued and not just a fleeting trend. Consider managers who show openness to flexible scheduling or who actively take mental health days themselves. Their actions provide employees with an unspoken permission to do the same, significantly impacting the organization's culture.

Training and development are also vital channels for initiating culture change. By offering workshops focused on developing skills such as time management, stress reduction, and effective communication, HR can empower employees at all levels to make choices that support balance. These educational opportunities should be ongoing rather than one-off events, reflecting the continuous nature of cultural evolution.

However, fostering such change is not without its challenges. Resistance is a natural reaction, particularly when it involves altering established norms and routines. Employees and managers may initially be skeptical or cautious about the new direction. It's essential for HR to address these concerns directly, providing clear communication about the benefits of a balanced culture and consistent support throughout the transition process.

Feedback mechanisms are crucial tools during this transformation. Establishing channels for employees to share their experiences—be they successes or struggles—ensures that the new cultural initiatives are being monitored, assessed, and refined in real-time. HR can facilitate forums for conversation, regular feedback surveys, or suggestion boxes that encourage candor. This dialogue helps in maintaining momentum and in tweaking strategies to better meet the needs of the workforce.

A major underpinning of effective cultural change is the alignment of policies and practices. It's not enough to talk the talk; companies must walk the walk. This means revisiting policies to ensure they reflect and reinforce the cultural shifts underway. Flexible working arrangements, comprehensive wellness programs, and policies that discourage overwork, like technology curfews, must be thoughtfully integrated into the organizational framework.

Moreover, recognition and reward systems should be adapted to reinforce the desired culture. Traditional metrics of success—such as long hours or rapid responses—may need rethinking. Instead, celebrating achievements that align with work-life harmony, like successful project completions within set hours or creative problem-solving in team settings, affirms the value of balance. These recognition efforts can be public, such as in newsletters or team meetings, to enhance their visibility and impact.

Ultimately, it's about creating a resilient culture that's capable of adapting over time. As the needs and expectations of the workforce evolve, so too should the company's approach to supporting its people. Regular assessments of and adjustments to the culture aren't just beneficial—they're necessary to ensure the company's core values remain aligned with employee well-being. This dynamic approach can help maintain a strong, engaged, and loyal workforce, which is essential for both organizational success and employee satisfaction.

In conclusion, encouraging organizational culture change towards better work-life harmony involves a dedicated, multi-faceted strategy. By assessing current norms, envisioning a balanced future, leading by example, investing in training, listening and responding to feedback, and aligning policies and practices with these shifts, HR professionals can lead their organizations into a new era where work complements life rather than competes with it. This shift not only benefits employees but enhances productivity, engagement, and retention, ultimately contributing to the overall success of the organization.

Chapter 12:
Personal Growth and Self-Care

As we journey through the evolving landscape of work and personal life, the focus on personal growth and self-care becomes more vital than ever. In this chapter, we dive into how prioritizing our own development and well-being can act as a cornerstone for achieving long-term balance. Embracing continuous learning is not just about acquiring new skills, but also expanding our mindset, opening doors we never thought possible. At the same time, self-care is a conscious effort to acknowledge and nurture our own needs—this isn't about fleeting indulgences, but about establishing sustainable habits that invigorate both mind and body. From mindfulness practices to setting aside time for passion projects, these acts of self-preservation foster resilience and adaptability. By consciously integrating these practices, individuals can better navigate the dynamic post-pandemic world, paving the way for a harmonious blend of professional success and personal fulfillment.

Prioritizing Personal Growth

In the ever-evolving landscape of work and life, the idea of personal growth isn't just an option; it's a necessity. As remote workers, entrepreneurs, and working parents, we find ourselves navigating a world where boundaries blur and demands intensify. Prioritizing personal growth amidst these challenges requires a deliberate focus, one that turns inward even while the outside world demands our constant attention.

Personal growth is, at its core, about becoming the best version of yourself. It's about enhancing your skills, expanding your knowledge, and cultivating qualities that not only improve your professional life but also enrich your personal well-being. In today's fast-paced environment, this journey isn't linear; it's a multifaceted path requiring intention and mindfulness.

Why, then, is personal growth so crucial? Firstly, it equips us with the resilience needed to handle unpredictabilities. In a post-pandemic world where the traditional work model is steadily shifting, the ability to adapt quickly is invaluable. Skills that push us out of our comfort zones foster this adaptability. Moreover, committing to personal development can lead to increased job satisfaction. When we actively work to improve ourselves, that effort often translates into a deeper sense of fulfillment in our roles.

But personal growth isn't just about acquiring new skills or even climbing the corporate ladder. It's profoundly personal and incorporates every facet of our lives, including mental and emotional health. Since the lines between work and life continue to blur, emotional intelligence becomes paramount. Understanding how to manage emotions — both our own and those of others — helps us maintain healthier relationships, better communication, and increased empathy, all of which are vital in remote and hybrid work settings.

A significant aspect of promoting personal growth is the willingness to set goals. Goals act as a roadmap, guiding us towards specific objectives and providing a sense of direction. These goals should be diverse, covering professional aspirations, personal ambitions, and even health-related targets. Achieving a balance among them is essential to ensure that personal growth isn't skewed in favor of one particular area.

For remote workers and entrepreneurs, time management and self-discipline are essential skills to cultivate. The flexibility offered by remote work, though beneficial, can lead to procrastination without a disciplined approach. Implementing strategies such as time blocking or the Pomodoro Technique can help maintain focus and productivity while also allocating time for personal development activities.

Incorporating feedback is another important practice. Constructive criticism should be sought actively and welcomed with open arms, not just from peers but also mentors. Feedback provides insights into areas that need improvement and highlights strengths to build upon. This continuous loop of feedback and improvement is a core component of personal growth.

Moreover, cultivating curiosity keeps the journey of personal growth vibrant and exciting. It fosters a mindset of lifelong learning, encouraging us to experiment and indulge in activities that might seem outside our professional scopes — be it learning a new language, taking up a hobby, or exploring varied cultures. Each experience enriches our perspectives, subsequently enhancing our adaptability and problem-solving skills.

Mindfulness practices, like meditation or yoga, can underpin personal growth. They teach us to remain present and aware, which helps in managing stress and nurturing a calm mind. Regular mindfulness practice can enhance focus, creativity, and resilience, all vital attributes for anyone striving for growth.

Lastly, never underestimate the power of rest and reflection. Growth doesn't always mean action; sometimes, it's about pausing. Reflect on experiences, assess achievements against goals, and recalibrate where necessary. That reflective pause is as important as the forward motion on the growth journey, ensuring the changes align with our core values and long-term vision.

Prioritizing personal growth isn't a one-off task but a continuous journey. It demands daily commitment, a balance between striving and reflecting, and a harmonious blend of action and rest. By weaving growth into the fabric of our everyday lives, we don't just benefit professionally; we truly thrive as individuals.

Self-Care Practices for Long-Term Balance

Long-term balance in our fast-paced lives hinges on consistent self-care practices that align with our personal and professional aspirations. It's essential to build a routine that is both flexible and sustainable, accommodating the unpredictable nature of modern work environments. By blending physical activities with moments of mindfulness, individuals can nurture their mental and emotional health. Regular exercise, even in short bursts, boosts energy and focus, while practices like meditation and journaling provide clarity and calm amid chaos. Cultivating a supportive community, both online and offline, enhances resilience and motivation, offering a safe space to exchange ideas and encouragement. Prioritizing sleep, hydration, and nutrition lays a foundation for vitality, enabling a robust response to daily challenges. Ultimately, the integration of these self-care rituals into our daily lives doesn't just foster well-being; it becomes a source of strength and inspiration, fostering creativity and perseverance as we navigate the ever-evolving demands of our personal and professional spaces.

Online Review Request for This Book We'd be grateful if you could take a moment to share your thoughts on how "Self-Care Practices for Long-Term Balance" has enriched your journey toward achieving a harmonious work-life blend, helping others discover the transformative insights within.

Conclusion

In navigating the labyrinth of modern work environments, achieving a harmonious work-life balance has emerged as more than just an aspiration—it's a necessity. The journey we've undertaken in this book was not just about identifying challenges but also uncovering actionable strategies that cater to diverse roles and situations. Whether you're a remote worker adjusting to a decentralized office, a parent juggling multiple responsibilities, an entrepreneur driven by passion, or a leader fostering team support, the principles outlined here aim to enrich your professional and personal realms.

As we conclude, it's crucial to recognize that work-life balance isn't a one-size-fits-all concept; it's a highly personal journey defined by individual needs and circumstances. Embracing this diversity means acknowledging your unique path. By understanding work-life balance's core ideals, as discussed in the initial chapters, you're better equipped to tailor a lifestyle that harmonizes your work obligations with personal aspirations. The importance of this balance extends beyond personal well-being, influencing broader organizational health and societal norms.

The pandemic thrust many into the world of remote work, reshaping the traditional office confines forever. With this shift, setting boundaries has never been more pertinent. The rhythm between employment duties and life's other facets needs thoughtful delineation. Establishing strong boundaries isn't about restriction; it's about freedom. Knowing when to close your laptop or take that mindful pause can enhance productivity and emotional reserves. As such, it's vital to communicate your boundaries clearly, ensuring mutual respect in professional relationships.

Stress, needless to say, remains an inevitable companion in today's fast-paced world. However, identifying and managing it is within our repertoire. Practical techniques for stress reduction discussed earlier, such as mindfulness practices and effective time management, become indispensable tools. These stress management techniques serve not just as remedies but as preventive measures. Implementing them proactively can help avert burnout, fostering resilience and vigor.

Amidst these strategies, the role of technology is a double-edged sword. On one hand, it offers remarkable tools for enhancing efficiency and maintaining connections; on the other, it can lead to burnout if not judiciously managed. Leveraging technology to maintain balance involves conscious decision-making about its usage, drawing clear lines between digital engagement and withdrawal. By doing so, you can safeguard your mental bandwidth and focus for what truly matters.

It's essential to highlight the unique challenges faced by working parents, who balance professional expectations with the demands of parenting. This dual responsibility can be overwhelming without adequate support systems. Encouragingly, as discussed in the book, there are solutions available through flexible work arrangements and community support. These resources empower parents to fulfill both their familial and occupational roles effectively.

Entrepreneurs and leaders, on the other hand, face the challenge of sustaining passion without succumbing to exhaustion. Here, maintaining balance becomes a strategic priority for long-term success. For entrepreneurs, this means infusing passion with prudence, avoiding the pitfall of overcommitment. Leaders, meanwhile, must champion an environment that supports work-life balance for their teams through exemplary leadership and empathetic management policies.

Human Resources (HR) professionals play a pivotal role in shaping an organizational culture that prioritizes balance. The policies and practices they implement serve as the scaffolding for employees' well-being. HR's proactive stance on fostering this culture through supportive policies and dialogue leads to healthier workplaces and higher employee satisfaction levels.

Finally, at the heart of sustaining balance is personal growth and self-care. Investing in oneself, prioritizing growth, and embracing self-care rituals offer profound benefits. Self-awareness leads to more informed choices that align with long-term balance goals. Prioritizing these aspects ensures you're equipped not only for professional challenges but also for life's unpredictable turns.

As we close this exploration, it's apparent that work-life balance isn't merely an endpoint but a dynamic, ongoing process. It's about continuous adaptation, conscious choices, and personal agency. Let this journey serve as a guide but remember, the path is yours to carve. As you craft your narrative, may balance be your ally and guide you toward a fulfilling, joyous life.

Appendix A: Resources and Further Reading

As you embark on the journey toward achieving a fulfilling work-life balance, it's essential to have a portfolio of resources at your disposal. The following list is curated to provide further insights and practical strategies that complement the themes discussed throughout this book. These resources include books, articles, podcasts, and websites that have been influential in the realm of balancing professional aspirations with personal well-being. They cater to remote workers, entrepreneurs, working parents, managers, HR professionals, and anyone seeking to thrive in today's dynamic work environment.

Books

"**The 4-Hour Workweek**" **by Timothy Ferriss** - Offers unconventional strategies to streamline work and create more time for life's pleasures.

"**Dare to Lead**" **by Brené Brown** - Explores the power of vulnerability in leadership and how it contributes to creating a balanced and brave workspace.

"**Essentialism: The Disciplined Pursuit of Less**" **by Greg McKeown** - Focuses on discerning what is essential and eliminating the rest to achieve a more balanced and meaningful life.

Articles

"Why Remote Work Thrives in Some Companies and Fails in Others" by Ryan Holmes - This article examines the critical components that make remote work successful.

"The Futility of Chasing Work-Life Balance" by HBR - Discusses how chasing the perfect balance may be less effective than integrating work and life strategically.

Podcasts

"WorkLife with Adam Grant" - Offers insights on making work not suck, exploring topics that matter to remote workers and entrepreneurs alike.

"The Tim Ferriss Show" - Features diverse guests and their strategies for balance, productivity, and well-being.

Websites and Online Resources

Mind Tools - Stress Management - Provides tools and resources for managing stress effectively in various work scenarios.

Remote.co - A wealth of articles and advice specifically aimed at remote workers and companies transitioning to remote work.

Well-being Apps

Headspace - A user-friendly meditation app perfect for integrating relaxation into daily routines.

Todoist - An excellent tool for task management that can help you allocate time efficiently and prioritize personal well-being.

Harmony at Hand

While technology and modern solutions present opportunities for maintaining balance, it's crucial to remember the importance of personal reflection and self-care. As you explore these resources, allow yourself to adjust and adapt strategies to fit your unique lifestyle and goals. Remember, the journey to work-life balance is personal, and what works for one individual may not be suitable for another. Keep experimenting and discovering what aligns best with your life objectives.

www.ingramcontent.com/pod-product-compliance
Lightning Source LLC
Chambersburg PA
CBHW032047290426
44110CB00012B/991